PENTLAND HERO

Born of a maritime family, Roy Pedersen's former
career with development agencies HIDB and HIE,
where he pioneered numerous innovative and successful ventures, have given him a matchless insight
into world shipping trends and into the economic
and social conditions of the Highlands and Islands.
He is now an author, proprietor of a cutting edge
consultancy and an SNP Highland councillor.

PENTLAND HERO

THE SAGA OF THE ORKNEY SHORT SEA CROSSING

Roy N. Pedersen

BIRLINN

First published in 2010 by
Birlinn Limited
West Newington House
10 Newington Road
Edinburgh
EH9 1QS

www.birlinn.co.uk

2

ISBN: 978 1 84158 888 9

British Library Cataloguing-in-Publication Data
A catalogue record for this book is available from the British Library

Typeset by Iolaire Typesetting, Newtonmore
Printed and bound by CPI Cox & Wyman Ltd, Reading

This book is dedicated to the Banks family

Somebody said it couldn't be done,
But he with a chuckle, replied
That, 'maybe it couldn't, but he'd be the one
Who wouldn't say no till he tried.'
So he buckled right in with a trace of a grin
On his face. If he worried he hid it.
He started to sing as he tackled the thing
That couldn't be done, and he did it.

Edgar A. Guest, from *Collected Verse*, 1934

CONTENTS

List of Illustrations

Pentalina arriving at Gills Bay.

The Swilkie.

Andrew Banks recounts his story to the author.

The first long serving *St Ola* (1892–1951).

Blockships in Holm Sound and the start of the barrier's construction.

Churchill Barrier No. 3 today.

The second *St Ola* (1951–1975) discharging a car by derrick at Stromness in August 1962.

The third *St Ola* as new in 1975, the first RO-RO ferry on the Pentland Firth.

Messrs Thomas & Bews' *Pentland Venture* at John O'Groats.

Varagen on the day she was named by Lisa Tullock in 1989.

Pentalina B at St Maragret's Hope.

Placing the 'H' beam between the Gills Bay dolphins.

Dredging at Gills Bay.

The floating dock extension to Gills Bay pier with Stroma in the background.

NorthLink *Hamnavoe* arriving at Scrabster.

Claymore at Gills Bay in February 2009. The floating dock extension, with digger on top, is on the right.

Resplendent *Pentalina* just after launching at Cebu.

Pentalina's controls. Note the four throttles to the right of the stack.

Pentalina at her home port of St Margaret's Hope.

FOREWORD

by Lord George Robertson

This is a book that will doubtless scandalise. It is the story of how the islands of Scotland, the subject of noisy and wholly justified championing over the years, have in fact been betrayed by the very authorities they trusted to protect their vital connectivity with the mainland. It is also a story, as yet unfinished, of how the taxpayer has for many years artificially shored up inefficient, inappropriate, over-expensive ferry services where in many cases there have been cheaper, efficient, subsidy-free alternatives.

The book chronicles a classic example of how one man had the tenacity, the resources, the persistence and public-minded spirit to provide a ferry service for his fellow citizens between his native Orkney Islands to the nearest part of the Scottish mainland. It is a tale of governmental skulduggery, unfair competition and elected authoritarianism – all designed to drive him from his dream of a better and cheaper service for the public. And all of it organised and orchestrated by the very people, in Edinburgh and Kirkwall, elected to look after the islanders' interests.

It is, of course, not the only saga of how the islanders of Scotland have been short-changed by their elected masters. How the iconic Caledonian MacBrayne, the subject of countless sentimental documentaries and misty-eyed stories, has under-mined every other innovator in the name of so-called 'lifeline' services is a story yet to be written. This state-owned entity almost unbelievably manages to make a loss on every single route it operates. And it has kept that fact a closely guarded secret from the public which owns it for over half a century. It has then used the ignorance of that fact to claim that any private operator would cherry-pick its routes, thus eliminating an assumed but wholly imaginary cross-subsidy.

CalMac, as it is now known, drove a private operator, Western Ferries, off the route to the whisky island of Islay in the 1980s by undercutting the private operator's prices using taxpayers' cash. CalMac beat P&O in the tender for the Orkney route in the 1990s, and then when their tender-winning bid turned out to be completely unrealistic, was allowed to re-tender and, even more astonishingly, awarded the new tender with even more taxpayers' cash funding the whole dismal episode.

And all the time Andrew Banks, no predatory maritime mogul but an Orkney-born and bred public-spirited entrepreneur, found obstacles, not subsidy; hostility, not cooperation; and a cash-rich competitor with limitless funds. He also faced a local authority which constantly favoured the state-owned ferry's longer route and opposed the shorter crossing. Orkney Islands Council have now publicly admitted that they refused him access to a council-owned pier to constrain his enhanced services.

How Andrew Banks and his family battled these odds, and prevailed, is the stuff of legend, and reflects a determination and entrepreneurial spirit of which all of Scotland should be proud. This book tells the story of one man fighting an industrial bully. It amplifies the lone voice of the consumer against the battalions of 'we-know-best' government monopolists, who have never turned in anything approaching a profit. It documents Andrew Banks's epic journey to the Far East to build and sail back the custom-built ferry for the St Margaret's Hope to Gills Bay route. It is not only a modern adventure story, but also the heart-warming tale of how he faced down government opposition, unfair competition and fate itself. Here is an inspiring story of a man who simply refuses to give up.

Just how much public money was used to compete with Andrew Banks is still to be disclosed. The secrecy with which Caledonian MacBrayne shrouds its costs and taxpayer generosity defies understanding or calculation. But it runs into many millions of pounds, resources direly needed elsewhere in the country, and especially the islands. That in itself is a scandal. But now, through Roy Pedersen's careful research and disclosure in this book, the taxpayers of Scotland can get a glimpse of the inconvenient truths hidden under the Caledonian MacBrayne carpet, and the feeble acquiescence of the generations of Scottish Ministers who allowed them to be brushed there.

(Lord) George Robertson is a former Secretary of State for Defence and Secretary General of NATO. He was also Shadow Secretary of State for Scotland and a Labour Member of Parliament for 21 years. He is now a Non-Executive Director of Western Ferries (Clyde) Ltd – which operates an usubsidised ferry service between Dunoon, where he was brought up, and Gourock. In competition with heavily subsidised CalMac, it carries nearly 90 per cent of the traffic on the route.

PREFACE

Just before Christmas 2008, a brand new futuristic, super-efficient catamaran ferry arrived in Orkney. Her like had never been seen before in Scotland. She was *Pentalina*, flagship of Pentland Ferries, a private company owned by a quietly spoken Orkney farmer's son, Andrew Banks. The new ship was and is remarkable enough, but the story of how Andrew Banks was able to establish the long sought 'short sea crossing' between Orkney and the Scottish mainland in the face of a concerted and sustained campaign by well-funded public bodies to undermine his enterprise, is on the one hand a miracle and on the other an outrage. This book describes that David-and-Goliath struggle.

When he faced mighty Philistine Goliath, lone David won the day with clear thinking, simple but effective technology and right on his side. While the state sector poured vast sums of public money into new terminals and extravagant ships that required unbelievably large subsidy to maintain the time-served but longer, more exposed, Pentland Firth crossing, Andrew Banks had a different approach. With a tiny team of trusted colleagues and without a penny of public funds, he built terminals and started operating the new frequent, cheap, short route on a viable basis with two old ferries pensioned off from state operator Caledonian MacBrayne, all for a tiny fraction of the cost of the state-subsidised operation. In so doing he opened up access between Orkney and mainland Scotland as never before, and was awarded the title of 'Orkney Citizen of the Year'.

It might be thought that such an achievement would have won Pentland Ferries the support of the powers that be, but no.

Obstacle after obstacle was put in the way to frustrate the new enterprise. It is a testament to Andrew Banks's tenacity and strength of character that the short sea crossing between St Margaret's Hope and Gills Bay was created at all and that it became the success and the asset to Orkney it has. Such was Andrew's faith in the project that he was able to order the construction and delivery of the new *Pentalina*. That process in itself was not without its nightmarish aspects, but now she is on station, *Pentalina* and the short sea crossing are already harbingers of how more efficient Scottish ferry services may be organised in future.

It might also be thought that the kind of official obstruction experienced by Andrew Banks was a unique anomaly in an otherwise competent public administration of the country's ferry operations. In fact, Andrew's experience reflects a deep-rooted and longstanding malaise in the way the Scottish state-owned ferry sector is feather-bedded so as to resist the introduction of more cost-effective methods by the private sector. The background to this deplorable state of affairs is set out in this book.

Above all, however, this is the story of an idea and of the man who made that idea a reality. I have called it *Pentland Hero*, for the struggle to make a success of the short sea crossing was heroic beyond measure. If it had taken place at an earlier time it would have been worthy of inclusion in that great corpus of Icelandic Sagas in which Orcadians featured prominently. I have no doubt the skalds would have called our story 'Andrew's Saga'.

ACKNOWLEDGEMENTS

A work of this nature would not have been possible without encouragement, advice and assistance from a large number of people. First and foremost of these are Andrew Banks and his wife Susan, joint proprietors of Pentland Ferries. Andrew and his heroic achievements form the principal focus of this book, but without the sustained support of Susan, it is doubtful if, against the difficulties he faced, he could have pulled off the ground-breaking advance in Scottish ferry practice that he did. Equally, without their hours of patient replies to my questions, there would be no story to tell. So to Andrew and Susan, very special thanks are owed.

Particular thanks are also due to a number of other individuals who contributed materially to building up a picture of how this extraordinary saga unfolded. Professor Alfred J. Baird, Head of the Maritime Research Group of Napier University's Transport Research Institute (TRI) has been throughout a wellspring of information on, and analysis of, worldwide shipping matters. An inspiration to me over many years, Alf has also been a key source of good advice to Andrew himself in the development of Pentland Ferries. Bill Mowat, Vice Chairman of Gills Harbour Committee, provided an invaluable inside track into the history of north-east Caithness, the more recent development of Gills Bay harbour and its fruitful relationship with Pentland Ferries. Similarly, Orkney Councillor Jim Foubister provided helpful insights into issues and developments on the Orkney side of the water, particularly with regard to St Margaret's Hope, where he is a member of the harbour trust. Stuart Ballantyne, CEO of Sea

Transport Corporation, not only designed the new Pentland Ferries flagship *Pentalina*, but provided revealing comparisons between best practice worldwide and the longstanding ineptitude of the Scottish state-funded ferry scene. To similar effect, Craig Patrick, Sales and Marketing Manager of FBMA Marine Inc., the shipyard that built *Pentalina*, also furnished telling information comparing ships of NorthLink and Pentland Ferries. In terms of certain civil service thinking in the former Scottish Executive, Kieran Nash, now Managing Director of Croí na Mara Marine and Human Resource Solutions provided some startling revelations. I must also express my gratitude to the publisher and editorial team at Birlinn, in the first place for having faith in the project and secondly for their very helpful advice in pulling the published product together.

There were many more, some of whom would no doubt prefer to remain anonymous, who I must thank, albeit in a collective manner, for providing gems of inside information that confirmed the existence of some of the dark forces at work in trying to undermine our hero's pioneering project.

Of course I also owe a huge debt of gratitude to authors of previous publications, papers, articles and blogs covering the people, places and sea-going vessels of the Pentland Firth, and these are listed in the Bibliography. To illustrate the main aspects of the story, it is fortuitous that it has been possible to source a representative range of good photographs, most of which have not previously been seen in print. Where possible the sources of these are acknowledged and my thanks are due to all who gave me permission to include these images.

Finally, I must thank Marie Kilbride, who kindly agreed to proofread the various drafts as this work evolved. Every attempt has been made to ensure accuracy but on the basis that 'it is human to err', infallibility, while desired, is not guaranteed. The responsibility for any errors that may be found is, therefore, mine alone.

Roy N. Pedersen, Inverness, January 2010

LIST OF ABBREVIATIONS

BEA – British European Airways
BRDG – Bus Route Development Grant
CalMac – Caledonian MacBrayne
CSPCo – Caledonian Steam Packet Company
HIDB – Highlands and Islands Development Board
HITRANS – Highlands and Islands Transport Partnership
ITF – International Transport Workers' Federation
LMS – London Midland and Scottish Railway
LNER – London and North Eastern Railway
MCA – Maritime and Coastguard Agency
MSP – Member of the Scottish Parliament
NMC – Northern Maritime Corridor Group
OFT – Office of Fair Trading
OIC – Orkney Islands Council
RET – Road equivalent tariff
RoPax – RO-RO vehicle and passenger (vessel)
RO-RO – Roll-On/Roll-Off (ferry)
SEPA – Scottish Environmental Protection Agency
SETG – Scottish Executive Transport Group
SNP – Scottish National Party
SOLAS – The International Convention for Safety of
           Life at Sea
STAG – Scottish Transport Appraisal Guidance
STG – Scottish Transport Group

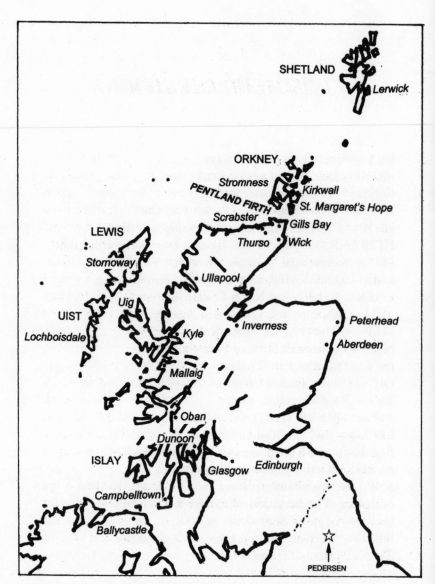

Scotland, showing principal places featuring in the text

1

WE MEET THE HERO

We're Orkney bound! As we drive north through Scotland's most northerly county of Caithness on the most northerly stretch of the Great North road we rise up the flank of Warth Hill, over a modest summit, and there in front of us is a glorious panorama: blue sea, studded with islands. This is the Pentland Firth, separating Scotland's north coast from the Orkney Islands. To the right, marking the eastern entrance to the Firth, is the Muckle Skerry, a flat rocky islet crowned by a pair of towers, one tall, slender lighthouse and the shorter remnant of its erstwhile twin. Left of that is the considerable green mass of South Ronaldsay, Orkney's most southerly inhabited island, just over six miles from the nearest point on the Scottish mainland. Further left still and more or less dead ahead are two more islands, smaller in size. The nearest and largest is Stroma, on which houses and other buildings can be discerned, and further away, quite near to the coast of South Ronaldsay, lies Swona. Behind Stroma, somewhat further away than South Ronaldsay, rise the steep brown hills of Hoy, whose name aptly means high island – Orkney's highest.

We are now almost at famed John O'Groats, but that is not our place of embarkation. We make a left turn and drive for about three miles westwards, parallel to the coast, past the settlement of Huna and on towards the little harbour at Gills Bay. Gills Bay, or Gills Haven, takes its name from two small ravines or clefts in an escarpment down which run two burns – the Big and Little Gibigill. These egress to the west and east of the harbour. As we approach, we look seaward and there, suddenly shooting out from behind Stroma, is our ferry, *Pentalina*, operated by Pentland Ferries. With her ram-bowed red and white twin hulls (for she is a state-of-the-art catamaran) and with her creaming wake, *Pentalina* presents a striking and purposeful air. Like some Greek war galley, she speeds towards Gills Bay terminal. We press on, turning right down a side road, to fetch up at the small boat harbour and ferry terminal in good time to check in before our ship berths.

The terminal facilities are basic but do the job. The building is flat-roofed, incorporating an office, waiting room and toilet facilities. Check-in couldn't be easier. We are already pre-booked and as we approach the generous marshalling area we are stopped by shore manager, Thomas Meikle, armed with clipboard. He looks at the car registration, checks our names and signals for us to join the queue of waiting vehicles. 'It's that fellow with the Norskie name,' we hear him declare to his colleague.

We have time enough to stretch our legs and look around. At the seaward end of the marshalling area is the link-span; the hinged bridge that connects the ferry's vehicle deck with the shore. Alongside the link-span and stretching northwards into the Firth is a long pier of curious construction. The pier is fenced off and littered with assorted heavy plant – clearly work in progress.

Pentalina turns and slides smartly, stern first, into position alongside the pier at one o' clock, dead on time. Heaving lines are thrown; she is made fast and the stern vehicle ramp unfolds onto the link-span. In no time a line of cars, motor-cycles, vans, bikes, passengers and heavy goods trailers stream ashore. We must hurry back to the car. It's time to board. As the queue moves forward, we are given the signal to proceed down the link-span and onto the vehicle deck, where a crewman directs us to our allotted space. We gather our togs and make our way up a companionway (stairs), past the entrance to one of the comfortable saloons to the promenade or sun deck, where we lean on the rail to contemplate our reason for being here.

This popular service, operated by Pentland Ferries between Gills Bay and St Margaret's Hope on South Ronaldsay, is the shortest, quickest, cheapest and most frequent vehicle ferry crossing between Orkney and the Scottish mainland. It is also the crossing least exposed to adverse weather conditions and is the creation of one remarkable man – Andrew Banks. With a very small team, and without a penny of public money, he built the terminals (virtually with his bare hands), sourced suitable vessels and commenced profitable operations against a sustained campaign of bureaucratic obstruction and heavily subsidised competition. Our mission is to meet up with Andrew and his wife Susan at St Margaret's Hope to hear their amazing story of how, against heavy opposition and with dogged determination, he succeeded where lesser men would undoubtedly have given up.

But first we have the passage to enjoy. *Pentalina* is ready to depart. The ramp is lifted, lines are slacked and cast off, engines throb and a creamy foam indicates that we are moving away from the link-span. As we gather way, the public address system blares out the safety announcement about muster stations, lifejackets and the signal for 'abandon ship'. This is, of course, no reflection on the security of *our* ship; it is a requirement by the Maritime and Coastguard Agency (MCA) of all passenger vessels when proceeding to sea. Once well clear of the pier, *Pentalina* surges forward at a fair lick and heads for Orkney.

Let's explore the ship. *Pentalina* is a fine ship and a particularly steady sea boat. She was specially designed for the route to Andrew Banks's specification. Built by the Balamban yard of FBMA Marine Inc. at Cebu in the Philippines, she was delivered in December 2008. In terms of Scottish ferries, *Pentalina* is revolutionary. Her twin hull configuration permits an unusually commodious vehicle deck in relation to her size. With her four engines and quadruple screws, she is fast, very manoeuvrable and fuel efficient; important attributes in times of high fuel costs. Each hull hosts comfortable covered seated passenger observation accommodation, purser's office, luggage space, toilets and the cosy cafeteria on the port side is a prime spot for a chat with fellow passengers over a snack. Above the covered accommodation is the broad open-air promenade deck, where a good all-round view may be enjoyed. In fact it's time for us to pay the passage fare at the purser's office before again going on to the promenade deck.

And what a view! It's a glorious, crisp, sunny spring day and we are now passing close to the west side of the island of Stroma with its low cliffs. For all its numerous houses Stroma, which belongs to the Caithness parish of Canisbay, is no longer inhabited. It once carried a population of 550, but the last family left in 1962. As we pass Stroma light at the north end of the island, the ship seems to slew involuntarily. This movement is caused by a meeting of strong swirling currents which are, as we look, clearly visible in the sea around us. There is no need to worry. Our skipper knows the Firth and its tricks and a swift adjustment to the helm brings us back on course. And now, on our starboard side, a large school of porpoises; some leaping right out of the water. They love to ride the wake of the ship and the cross-cutting currents. They're having a whale of a time!

There are about three miles of open water before we reach the lee of Swona. Swona, also now uninhabited, is the first of the Orkney Islands we encounter. The sharp-eyed among the passengers have spotted grey seals on the rocky shoreline and the cattle that we can see on Swona are feral, having been left to fend for themselves on the island since 1974. They are now recognised as a separate breed. The island cliffs abound with seabirds – puffins, fulmars, great skuas, razor bills, guillemots and gannets.

Northwards we steam along the coast of South Ronaldsay through the Sound of Hoxa between Hoxa Head, the western-most point on South Ronaldsay, and the island of Flotta, with its prominent flare stack. Flotta hosts a major oil transhipment terminal. On Hoxa Head itself, abandoned concrete gun emplacements and lookout posts are clearly visible on our starboard side. These now deserted towers protected the southern entrance to the great naval anchorage of Scapa Flow during the dark days of the Second World War.

Once round Hoxa Head, *Pentalina* turns to starboard and eastwards along the northern coast of South Ronaldsay, then starboard again round Needle Point, and we are in the snug bay of St Margaret's Hope with its delightful huddle of stone houses. *Pentalina* is swung through 180 degrees and backs gently alongside the pier. We are ushered down to the vehicle deck to take charge of our car and once the ship is securely berthed, and the stern ramp lowered, we drive ashore.

There, standing at the head of the link-span, is Andrew Banks.

We draw aside out of the traffic flow, get out, shake hands and exchange greetings. Andrew is not the archetypal shipping magnate. Wearing overalls and yellow 'rigger' working boots, he is well-built, quietly spoken; shy almost, but with an open face that perhaps belies strength of purpose. 'Would you like to come up to the house? We can talk there.'

Just then, across the road, we spot smiling Professor Alfred J. Baird, Head of Edinburgh's Napier University's Maritime Research Group – a longstanding friend, associate and ace analyst of shipping operations. More exchange of greetings and we all head for the nearby Banks family home, *Ceol na Mara*.

Andrew's wife Susan has prepared tea and scones for us. Susan is a pivotal figure in the planning and operation of the business as well as wife and mother to a family of four well-adjusted offspring. We take our ease. Andrew is an unassuming man, uncomfortable with fuss and formality, but among friends who have observed his achievements over the last decade he and Susan relate the saga of the genesis, development and ultimate success of Pentland Ferries. So the time has come to set the scene.

THE PENTLAND FIRTH AND
SEA TRAVEL LONG AGO

The Pentland Firth takes its name from the Old Norse *Petta-landsfjorðr*, or Pictland Firth, in other words, the arm of the sea that separated Viking Orkney from the land of the Picts to the south. In truth it is not a 'firth' at all but more correctly the 'channel' that separates the Orkney archipelago from Caithness in the Scottish mainland. It is about 17 miles (27 kilometres) in length from the Pentland Skerries in the east to Dunnet Head in the west. The shortest distance across the Firth, 6¼ miles (10 kilometres), is at its eastern end between Brough Ness on the Orkney island of South Ronaldsay and Duncansby Head at the extreme north-eastern point of Caithness and of Great Britain. To the north the Firth opens out to form the entrance to the extensive natural harbour of Scapa Flow. At its western end it narrows again somewhat before opening out to the Atlantic. Three islands lie astride the channel: the Muckle Skerry, the main constituent of the treacherous Pentland Skerries, marking the eastern approach, and then the islands of Stroma and Swona that form a line between Gills Bay and Herstan Head on the west coast of South Ronaldsay.

TIDE RACES, OVERFALLS AND WHIRLPOOLS

Reputed to be one of the most dangerous stretches of water in the world, this Firth is regarded among mariners with much respect. It is no coincidence, therefore, that there are four all-weather lifeboat stations close by. When the tide is on the flood, strong currents flow eastwards through the Firth with force. On the ebb, the tidal streams are reversed to flow westwards. This reversal occurs four times a day, and the accompanying effect of fierce eddies and over-falls can be exacerbated when a strong wind blows against the tide. These tidal conditions are among the world's most severe, and speeds of up to 16 knots have been recorded at the Firth's eastern extremity. The most extensive and dangerous tidal race in the Pentland Firth is 'The Merry Men of Mey' which occurs between St John's Point just over a mile (about 2 kilometres) north-west of Gills Bay in Caithness and Tor Ness on Hoy. The most turbulent section is over a sand wave field about 5½ miles (9 kilometres) west of Stroma. It is an odd quirk of nature that the waves formed by this most unpleasant over-fall form a natural breakwater, resulting in relatively calm water to the east of it and, even when the race is at its most violent, the Firth can be crossed to the east of the breakers in relatively smooth conditions. This phenomenon has a significant bearing on our story.

Another tide race at the north end of Stroma is known as 'the Swilkie'. It forms a violent swirling eddy to the east or west of Stroma, depending on the tide. According to Old Norse legend the Swilkie, meaning 'swallower', was caused by a huge magical quern called *Grotti* which endlessly ground salt to keep the seas salty. Besides the Swilkie itself, other highly visible races with over-falls and whirlpools form at Stroma and Swona so that vessels can suddenly be swung off course when crossing between eddy and fast-moving tide. Further east the 'Duncansby Race', 'The Bores of Duncansby' and the 'Liddel Eddy' can be violent and dangerous in certain conditions of wind and tide. The maps at Figs 1 and 2 show in diagramatic form the main flood and ebb tidal flows.

In the old days, for any ship passing through the Pentland Firth, a pilot well aquainted with the treacherous conditions was indispensable. The old Firth pilots were brave men of great skill from local seafaring families such as Mowat, Bremner and

Banks. The first recorded by name was one Finlay Mowat. On one occasion Finlay boarded an Orkney-bound vessel, only to discover too late that she was a pirate ship. The buccaneer vessel was subsequently apprehended and Finlay was lucky to escape trial and execution for piracy. Innocent though Finlay was in this instance, many of the Firth pilots were real characters, not averse to a little smuggling on the side.

Fig. 1: Flood tide during which powerful eddies form to the east of Stroma, Swona and the Pentland Skerrie. The main eddies are shown diagramatically by spirals

Fig. 2: Ebb tide during which the Merry Men of Mey (shown by wavy lines) are most active and eddies form to the west of Stroma and Swona

The consummate skill of the Pentland Firth pilots in riding the tide races and eddies avoided many a premature death. There were fatalaties, nonetheless, among those involved in this risky profession. Candlemass 1816 was the date of one such tragic event. On that day a group of Skirza pilots set out for Stromness in their now aging vessel to purchase a new six-oared pilot boat. Donald Bremner took command of the new boat. Prior to departure, Donald agreed to give passage home to some

Caithness men who had hoped but failed to get berths on one or other of the whaling ships that in those days called at Stromness. It took some time to get the passengers and their chests aboard. Meanwhile his colleague Andrew Bremner (or 'Aul Aunrie' as he later came to be known locally), taking advantage of the flood tide, set off for Caithness on the old boat, reaching Skirza safely. The delay in Donald's departure was to cost him dear. Donald and the prospective whalers in the new boat got caught in a strong west-flowing current that carried them towards Stroma and the dreaded Swilkie. As they rowed strongly to avoid the whirlpool, an oar broke. Observers on shore watched in horror as the new pilot boat was drawn into the Swilkie to be swallowed up, with the loss of all on board.

CROSSING THE FIRTH WITH OAR AND SAIL

For all the Pentland Firth's fearsome reputation, it has been crossed by men since the earliest times. The Neolithic people who, some 4,000 years ago, built Orkney's famed standing stones and the amazingly well-preserved village of Skara Brae, were undoubtedly skilled seafarers, for the archaeological evidence shows that they traded with peoples far to the south. What their boats were like, we do not know for sure, but they must have been sufficiently seaworthy to cope with cross-channel and coastal passages, no doubt by judiciously choosing favourable tidal and weather conditions for their voyages. Two thousand years later, the medieval records indicate that the Picts, who inhabited most of what is now Scotland north of the Forth, including Orkney and Caithness, had a powerful navy that ranged far and wide. Again, the Pentland Firth can't have presented any insuperable navigational barrier to them.

From about AD 800 onwards Pictish rule in Orkney and Caithness was broken by Viking hegemony. What they lacked in refined manners, these Norsemen made up for in vigour, courage and leadership qualities. The wonderful medieval

Icelandic *Orkneyinga Saga* (the Saga of the Orkneymen) vividly describes the dramatic, often bloody, sometimes pious, exploits of these Norse Orcadians and their jarls or earls, covering a period of some 300 years. Their manipulative skill brought Orkney a vast seaborne empire whose tentacles stretched from Dublin to Iceland and even, for a time, America. Of one Viking attribute there is no doubt: they were matchless seamen whether on their fighting longships or their trading 'knarrs'. The Pentland Firth was their highway to and from *Katanes* (Caithness), which was then an integral part of the earldom of Orkney.

Decline in the influence of the Norse earldom may be dated from events following the Battle of Largs in 1263 and the subsequent Treaty of Perth of 1266, whereby Magnus IV, King of Norway, 'granted, resigned and quit-claimed . . . for himself and his heirs forever, the Isle of Man with the rest of the Hebrides' in favour of Alexander III, King of Scots. Orkney, with Shetland, remained Norwegian possessions, but Scottish influence increased, particularly after 1379, when the Scottish Sinclair family inherited the earldom. The process was completed in 1469 by James III when he married Margaret, daughter of King Christian of Denmark and Norway. As is well known in Orkney, Christian was short of the funds for a dowry and pledged his lands and rights in Orkney (and Shetland) as security for the outstanding amount. King Christian never redeemed his pledge, and these northern isles remain part of Scotland to this day.

After the earldom came under Scottish jurisdiction, the Scandinavian connection declined in importance. Intermittent sea links, such as they were, tended to focus on the newly designated Scottish capital of Edinburgh and its port of Leith. In 1496, however, not long after the transfer to Scottish rule, a charter from William Sinclair, Earl of Caithness, was granted to one John Groat to operate a ferry between Caithness and Orkney. John Groat is sometimes styled 'Jan de Groot', as he was probably of a merchant family of Dutch origin. The Dutch connection is explicable, as the Sinclairs maintained strong trading links with Holland. The ferry's Caithness landing place in the estate of Duncansby and Warse in the parish of Canisby is still named John O'Groats after this pioneer ferryman. He set up his house adjacent to this Caithness landing and a flagpole marks the site. According to tradition, the dining room and dining table in John Groat's house were octagonal, so that neither his seven sons nor he himself had precedence at table. Where his wife sat is not recorded! John Groat is buried in Canisby churchyard. The motivation for establishing the ferry was doubtless the promotion by pious King James IV of a pilgrimage route to the shrine of St Magnus in Kirkwall, and the carriage of documents between the Edinburgh court and the earldom of Orkney. Remains of ecclesiastical buildings could once be traced at John O'Groats, where pilgrims would have stayed on making their passage across the Firth.

The documentary evidence suggests that the ferry operation between the Caithness coast around John O'Groats/Warse Haven and the nearest Orkney landfall at Burwick on South Ronaldsay was maintained continuously from John Groat's time onwards. The skill of the Pentland Firth ferrymen was renowned and, according to local belief, the Groats never lost a passenger. The last of the Groats engaged in the traffic was Malcolm Groat. He was financially ruined by Sinclair of Freswick, a particularly nasty and rapacious laird, who, around 1740, foreclosed on a debt of £8,352 17s 8d (Scots). The service continued in other hands and from the 1750s mails were conveyed weekly by six-oared open boat between Burwick and Huna, just over a mile west of John O'Groats, although in summer the ferry operated more frequently for passengers, weather permitting. The mode of operation was unusual. A boat set out from each side and the mails, passengers and other small items of goods were exchanged in mid-Firth, after which each boat would return to its home port. This strange arrangement had the merit of catching slack water and permitting each boat to return before the tide races and eddies built up full strength. A larger type of sailing craft was used to transport horses and cattle from Orkney.

Communication between the Scottish mainland and Orkney increased over the nineteenth century, largely due to improved economic conditions. By 1804 the mail frequency was increased to twice weekly and by the 1830s it was daily, weather permitting. A new road from Inverness to Wick and Thurso had enabled this increase in traffic, so that by 1819 a regular mail coach was leaving Inverness at 6 a.m. to reach Thurso by mid-day the following day. From there, however, the route became more difficult. The carriage road did not then reach Huna, so the Orkney mails had to be taken by foot from Wick and then ferried to Burwick, where a further walk to the north end of South Ronaldsay awaited, followed by a short but treacherous ferry-crossing to the island of Burray and a 2-mile walk north to the next ferry-crossing of Holm Sound before the Orkney mainland was reached. There then remained the final 7 miles overland to Kirkwall before the Orkney capital was finally reached. Stromness was, of course, another 15 or so miles distant by indifferent track. Latterly, the six-oared sailing yawl *Royal Mail* plied the Burwick–Huna mail and passenger route, supplemented as required by a larger boat with two sails and a jib. The map at Fig. 3 shows the sequence of ferries.

The last of the old style ferrymen was Peter Annal, born at Steen in South Ronaldsay in 1830. As a young man he joined the crew of the *Royal Mail*. His reward was sixpence a day as a 'hand', and one shilling if he carried half the mails on his back for the 9 miles from Burwick to Watersund at the northern end of South Ronaldsay. He served on the *Royal Mail* until 1858, when the service was superseded by a steamer service between Stromness and Scrabster. Peter, whose knowledge of the ways of the Firth was legendary, lived to the ripe old age of 93, departing this world in 1924. His grandson, the late Sandy

Annal, was able to pass on tales of the old ferry learned from his grandfather. Sandy described Peter in his old age, still enjoying a dram and a smoke of 'Black Twist' tobacco at his South Ronaldsay home thus: 'His favourite seat was at the table near the window. He could tell exactly how the tide was flowing any hour or day of the week, when to leave for Groats and which course to take.'

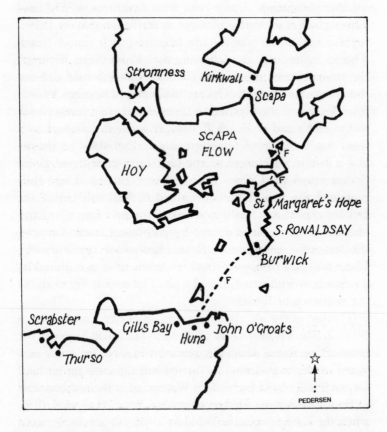

Fig. 3: The Pentland Firth mail ferries (indicated by 'F') in the days of oar and sail

For all its hurdles, the daily frequency of the short sea crossing gave Orkney its main means of urgent communication with the south in terms of mail and passenger movement. As the Orkney economy evolved, however, the islands' trade with the outside world developed mainly by means that for the most part avoided the Pentland Firth. By the eighteenth century, trading vessels exported bere (fast ripening barley) to Norway, Holland, the West Highlands and Ireland, whilst timber, coal and consumer goods were imported. Orkney was also astride the great circle route between continental European ports and North America. Kirkwall and Stromness became calling points. Stromness emerged as a centre for the Hudson's Bay Company and for Arctic whalers, with many Orcadians serving in both. The Pentland Firth remained hazardous for sailing vessels and many came to grief while attempting passage. Better charts and the construction of lighthouses lessened, but by no means eliminated, the navigational challenge that the Firth presented.

By the beginning of the nineteenth century Orkney had built up a regular and significant domestic trade with the Forth Ports and Leith in particular, and also with Liverpool, using sailing smacks. These smacks carried Orkney's exports and imports and were also the preferred mode for passengers even though schedules were intermittent, latterly about thrice monthly, and passage times variable.

STEAMSHIPS

Scotland pioneered steam navigation in Europe, and the emergence of this innovation was to revolutionise the pattern and magnitude of world trade. This was no less true in the case of Orkney. The first recorded passage through the Pentland Firth by a steamer was by a vessel called *Tug* in 1817. This craft bestowed her name as a generic for all powered vessels engaged in towage. In 1825 the steamer *United Kingdom* made the first summer seacruise by steamer from Clyde to Leith in 1825 via the Firth.

In December 1832 the steamer *Helensburgh* was chartered by the Crown Agents to take the general election poll-books to Orkney and Shetland. She made it with difficulty to Kirkwall, but was unfit to reach Shetland. The first scheduled passenger steamer service to Orkney was made by *Velocity*, of the Aberdeen, Leith, Clyde and Tay Shipping Company which, in June 1833, extended her fortnightly sailings from Leith, Aberdeen and Wick to Kirkwall. *Velocity*, a paddle steamer of but 112 feet in length, operated in summer only. In 1836 *Velocity* was superseded by the larger and faster *Sovereign* to provide a weekly summer service to Kirkwall, extended on alternate weeks to Lerwick. The winter service was maintained by the company's sailing packets. Indeed, by offering lower rates for freight and passengers, locally owned sailing smacks remained in operation for many decades, even after the introduction of year-round scheduled steamer services two decades later.

In time, these pioneering efforts evolved into a coherent network of year-round passenger, mail and cargo steamer services and from 1875, to reflect its sphere of operation, the company name was changed to the North of Scotland, Orkney and Shetland Steam Navigation Co., popularly known as the 'North Company' for short. The history of the North Co. and its fleet named after saints has been written by several fine authors and is not repeated here, but a flavour of the pattern of operation in the late Victorian period may be gleaned from the following summary of services:

Monday:
Aberdeen–Lerwick (direct)
Leith–Aberdeen, Stromness, Scalloway and west
    Shetland ports
Leith–Aberdeen, Wick and Thurso

Tuesday:
Leith–Aberdeen, St Margaret's Hope, Kirkwall and Lerwick

Thursday:
Aberdeen–Lerwick (direct)

Thursday or Friday
Leith–Aberdeen and Wick

Friday
Leith–Aberdeen, Kirkwall and Lerwick

The North Co. also ran two 'local' services. One of these was from Lerwick to the North Isles of Shetland; the other ran across the Pentland Firth. The latter has an important bearing on the story of Andrew Banks's achievement.

3

THE PENTLAND FIRTH MAIL STEAMERS

The Town Council of Stromness had agitated for a steamer link with Caithness as early as 1832 but nothing came of that. The mails would still cross the Pentland Firth in the time-honoured fashion by open boat between Huna and Burwick for some time yet. The construction in 1852 of a pier for the export of flagstones at Scrabster, about 2 miles north-west of Thurso, and connecting road to that town provided the stimulus for action. Thurso was the terminus of the road and mail coach from the south. In this new circumstance, Scrabster with its pier became a more attractive transfer point for mail than the long walk to the exposed and undeveloped landing place at Huna. All that was needed was a vessel capable of the longer and more open Firth crossing between the new port and a suitable Orkney landfall.

A year later, in 1853, Alexander Sinclair, 13th Earl of Caithness (and Laird of Mey), drafted plans for a harbour at Gills Bay, then commonly known as Gills Haven, a couple of miles west of Huna, but they were never developed. Some years later his son James, the 'mechanical earl', built Phillips' Harbour at Harrow (a site some miles further west), for the export of flagstones, but by this time Scrabster had become the Caithness port for the new steamship service across the Pentland Firth.

The vessel was provided by a Stromness shipbuilder, John Stanger, who built the 81-foot wooden steamer *Royal Mail* in 1856 and, after engines and paddles had been installed, operated her between Stromness and Scrabster, daily except Sundays in summer and three times a week in winter. The little steamer was cunningly named, for Stanger had been able to wrest the mail contract from the old Huna–Burwick open boat operation, whose vessel was also, of course, called *Royal Mail*.

On the new steamer service, the combined revenue from carrying mails, passengers and goods made the operation a paying proposition. This first powered ferry service across the Pentland Firth was undoubtedly a welcome improvement to communication between Orkney and Caithness. Of course, adverse weather conditions affected the reliability of such a small and low-powered vessel, especially in winter. Nevertheless, the *Royal Mail* braved the crossing for 12 years and during that time carried out a number of rescues of crews and passengers from foundered vessels.

In 1867, the Post Office advertised a new mail contract. Three route options from mainland Scotland were offered:

Scrabster–Stromness
Gills Bay–Scapa
Scrabster–Scapa

These alternatives are interesting, and each has its pros and cons. Firstly Huna–Burwick (South Ronaldsay) was absent as an option, presumably because, although it offered the shortest crossing to an Orkney landfall, South Ronaldsay was at the extremity of a chain of islands, necessitating two further ferry crossings before Orkney Mainland was reached. And as noted earlier, Huna, which is at the extreme east end of Gills Bay, was undeveloped as a port and was well off the mail-coach route.

Scrabster–Stromness had become the established route. Scrabster was the only port on the north Caithness coast with a proper pier that additionally offered a more or less direct connection with the Thurso mail coach; Stromness had emerged as a significant port and trading centre and the road between Stromness and Kirkwall was now capable of taking wheeled vehicles. The downside was that this route was potentially the most exposed to difficult sea conditions. This disadvantage could to some extent be ameliorated by going either east or west about Hoy, depending on weather conditions. Going to the east through Scapa Flow offered a relatively sheltered passage for the northern half of the passage but necessitated crossing the treacherous Merry Men of Mey for the southern part of the passage across the Firth itself. Going to the west of Hoy avoided the Merry Men of Mey but left the vessel exposed to prevailing westerly winds, a lee shore and the full force of Atlantic swells.

The Gills Bay–Scapa option was the shortest of the Post Office's three options and would have removed most of the exposure problems, because this crossing was to the east of and, therefore, to a fair degree protected by, the breakwater effect of the Merry Men of Mey. Advantage could also be taken of the shelter offered by the islands of Stroma and Swona by going west or east thereof depending on wind and tide direction, so that the passage through open water was quite short, the rest of the route being in the relative shelter of Scapa Flow. Scapa itself is only 2 miles across a narrow isthmus from the Orkney capital of Kirkwall – about the same distance as Scrabster from Thurso. Scapa, however, lacked a pier. Gills Bay, on the Caithness side, and 1½ miles west of Huna, offered reasonable shelter but, like Huna, also had no proper pier.

It is no secret that a fierce rivalry existed between Kirkwall and Stromness, as remains the case today, and debate and argument as to the relative merits of the different options for crossing the Pentland Firth has raged on and off from that day till this. At that time it was the Scrabster–Stromness option that was to prevail, with George Robertson securing the £1,300 *per annum* mail contract. In April 1868 he took over the route with a tiny and inadequate chartered steamer, *Willington*, to be followed in quick succession by his tug *Petra* and then the following spring by his purpose-built 103-foot screw steamer *Express*. By modern standards, a small vessel for such a potentially rough crossing; but certainly an improvement on the *Royal Mail*.

It should be borne in mind that in those days overland travel on foot or horseback to and from the far north of Scotland was slow, and, in the case of the mail coach, both uncomfortable and expensive. By comparison, the developing steamer services between Orkney and the important Scottish centres of Aberdeen and Leith offered, by the standards of the time, speedy and reliable conveyance of passengers and goods. Thus the Pentland Firth crossing was then merely a low-volume local concern.

THE COMING OF THE RAILWAY

The balance was starting to shift, however. The Highland Railway was pushing north and by 1874 it had reached Thurso. The railway henceforth replaced the mail coach, offering a quicker and more comfortable journey between Inverness and the north. An improvement certainly, but this was no Victorian 'bullet train'! The journey between Thurso and Inverness took between six and nine hours, with innumerable stops. After changing trains at Inverness, Perth was a further six to seven and a half hours away, then it was another two to three hours to Edinburgh or Glasgow. All in all, when the Pentland Firth crossing and Kirkwall–Stromness road journey were added in, the 'overland' trip between the Orkney and Scottish capitals took the best part of 24 rattling and at times very cold hours. The Scrabster route, therefore, offered no real time advantage over the long steamer route to Aberdeen and Leith. With the comfort of a warm saloon, hearty meals and, for first-class passengers, a state room and sleeping berth for the night, that option remained the preferred one for most travellers.

Notwithstanding this, Orkney clearly offered a prospect of profit for the Highland Railway and in 1877 it sought and gained powers to operate steamers under the Highland Railway Steam Vessels Act of that year. In anticipation of this, the railway company had ordered a new, commodious steamer which they named *John o' Groat*. This new vessel, which replaced the *Express*, was faster, at 13½ knots, and much larger than any previous vessel on the route – too large and extravagant, it transpired, for she consistently lost the company money despite the mail contract revenue. This was not to be the last time an excessive provision on the route was to cause financial embarrassment.

In 1880 a new pier was built at Scapa, which thereafter became the main transfer point for the mail to and from Scrabster, and a twice-weekly onward connection to Stromness was also provided. As losses mounted, however, the Highland Railway wanted out and in 1882, the North of Scotland, Orkney and Shetland Steam Navigation Co. took on the route.

The North Co. replaced the *John o'Groat* with a new but much more economical raised quarterdeck screw steamer, *St Olaf*. This ship lasted on the route for eight years but the quest for economy brought with it a penalty. She had insufficient power to cope with the fast tide races met with on the Firth and she was sold in 1890. Two years later (having used chartered vessels in the meantime) the North Co. brought a new purpose-built steamer, *St Ola*, onto the route. This sturdy vessel was to become an Orkney institution, serving the same route for no fewer than 59 years. *St Ola*, at 135 feet, was not much longer than *St Olaf*, but was more stoutly built and had the reserve of power necessary for her demanding station. All in all she was a remarkable little ship.

St Ola's schedule varied over her long career, but the basic pattern was to remain the same for over half a century. Her home port was Stromness, whence she called at Scapa Pier for the mails and Kirkwall passengers, with a further stop off Hoxa, South Ronaldsay to meet a flit boat from St Margaret's Hope, and thence to Scrabster and the connection with the south train. The map at Fig. 4 shows the route. The pattern was reversed for the return journey.

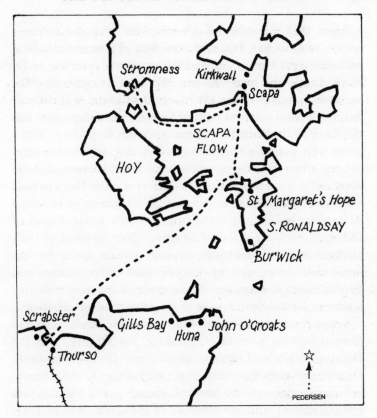

Fig. 4: The Scrabster route prior to the Second World War

GILLS BAY PIER

The loss of a direct sailing from north-east Caithness was deeply felt locally and as early as 1867 Gills Bay was seen to offer advantages over Scrabster as a possible Caithness port for the Orkney mail steamer, since it offered the prospect of a shorter and more sheltered passage to Scapa. There was indeed an old saying among Pentland Firth seamen: 'If you can cross the Firth; you can always land at Gills.' But the fundamental problem was that Gills lacked a pier and a rail connection.

From 1873 a number of schemes were proposed to run a railway to Gills Bay, but none bore fruit. There was also local pressure to get a pier built, and this cause was taken up by Dr Gavin Clark, the then Crofters MP for Caithness. In 1905, under the auspices of the 1897 Congested Districts (Scotland) Act, a 130-yard pier was built at Gills. A year later a pier was also built at St Margaret's Hope on South Ronaldsay. These works were part of a programme to help diversify the economy of areas where crofting agriculture could not support the local population. To manage the new facility a Gills Bay Harbour Committee was formed to 'manage Gills Harbour on behalf of all persons residing in the district of Gills in the Parish of Canisbay', with the object of ensuring 'that the fabric of Gills Harbour and its immediate environs remain intact for the foreseeable future and to promote such improvements and developments as necessary to encourage commerce, trade, industry and employment at or in the vicinity of the Harbour'.

Consent was granted to extend the new pier under a second phase to create a 'steamer terminus' for Orkney, and the Highland Railway Company proposed a 17-mile branch to Dunnet and Gills Bay, with direct connection to the steamer, but construction of the planned second phase and rail link was abandoned with the outbreak of the Great War in 1914. Towards the end of that war, the local community investigated the use of ex-military track to construct a railway branch to the pier, but this was vetoed by the government. For the next 60-odd years the Gills Bay pier languished as simply a haven for a few local small boats, but the community basis of its constituted body remained in place, enabling the momentous events that later led to its development as a viable ferry terminal (see Chapter 7).

4

THE WORLD WARS AND
THEIR LEGACY

With the outbreak of the First World War, Orkney suddenly found itself sitting on a major strategic asset – the vast sheltered natural harbour of Scapa Flow, which was, for the duration of hostilities, designated as the anchorage of the Royal Navy's Grand Fleet. The requirement for supplies and personnel movement generated by naval activity in that period created a hitherto unheard-of volume of traffic across the Pentland Firth which, with its Thurso rail link to and from the south, minimised threat from U-boat attack. The sterling efforts of the wee *St Ola* were supplemented by the North Co.'s *St Ninian*, which ran between Scrabster and the main naval base of Long-hope.

As is well known, after the armistice was declared the German High Seas Fleet was instructed to proceed to Scapa Flow to surrender to the British authorities. But as a face-saving gesture, the German commander, Admiral Ludwig von Reuter, gave the defiant and dramatic order to scuttle the fleet, with the result that 59 German warships were sunk. The ensuing salvage operation was to create a significant industry in post-World War I Orkney, and more recently the remaining wreckage of the German fleet has become an increasingly popular form of tourism with recreational scuba divers.

In 1919 Scapa Flow lost its status as the fleet's main base and in the ensuing two decades of peace, *St Ola*'s operational life returned to something like its pre-war normality. Two trends were beginning to emerge, however, that would eventually alter the balance among transport modes. The first was the motor car, and its derivatives the motor bus and motor lorry, which in the post-war period progressed from playthings of the rich and/or eccentric to become a credible means of getting around and delivering goods for a growing section of the general population. Then, in May 1934, Captain Edward Fresson started his pioneering Highland Airways air service between Inverness and Orkney, the first regular airmail service within the United Kingdom. Passenger numbers were then small, but his entre-preneurial genius built up an efficient unsubsidised business, and a future of popular air travel beckoned.

Normality was again disrupted by the second great conflict of Hitler's war. Scapa Flow resumed its role as a major naval base and, as before, *St Ola*'s sailings were supplemented by North Co.'s *St Ninian* and also by the elderly Shetland North Isles mail steamer *Earl of Zetland*. For a period at the peak of wartime activity this threesome was further complemented at different times by Scandinavian steamers: the Faroese *Tjaldur* and the Norwegian *Galtesund*. The latter had been seized by Norwegian freedom fighters in German-occupied Norway in 1942 and sailed to Shetland to join the Allied cause.

This time the tragedy of war was to leave a major and beneficial long-term legacy; a legacy that would open up a new post-war opportunity for the much shorter sea crossing between Orkney and Caithness that is the subject of this book. The main southern and western entrances to Scapa Flow were protected by booms to prevent entry by enemy vessels, espe-cially U-boats. Entry to the east of the great anchorage was blocked by the islands of North Ronaldsay and Burray, plus the lesser islets of Grims Holm and Lamb Holm. To stop up the shallow channels between each of these islands and Orkney Mainland, block-ships (obsolete and disposable vessels) were sunk in line to act as a barrier to entry. Unfortunately, that barrier was not watertight.

On the night of 13 October 1939, while the battleship HMS

Royal Oak was at anchor in Scapa Flow, the German U-boat *U-47*, under the command of Günther Prien, made a daring entry into the Flow through the narrow channel of Kirk Sound between Lamb Holm and Orkney Mainland. By skilful navigation and capitalising on the increased depth of water caused by a high spring tide that night, Prien was able to squeeze through a gap between the two block-ships *Soriano* and *Numidian*. Once through the makeshift barrier, he located the great battleship and launched a torpedo attack, as a result of which the *Royal Oak* was sent to the bottom in a matter of minutes. Prien then made his escape back through Kirk Sound to return to Nazi Germany and a hero's welcome. Of the *Royal Oak*'s 1,400-man crew, 833 were lost and the wreck is now a protected war grave.

THE CHURCHILL BARRIERS

After this catastrophe, Winston Churchill, then still First Lord of the Admiralty, ordered the construction of a series of permanent causeways to block the eastern approaches to Scapa Flow. Pending construction, three further block-ships were immediately sunk in Kirk Sound. For the remainder of the hostilities 1,300 Italian prisoners of war, who had been captured in North Africa, undertook the construction of what became known as the Churchill Barriers. The barriers join the islands together linking South Ronaldsay for the first time physically with Orkney Mainland, such that it became possible to drive from Kirkwall to South Ronaldsay's most southerly point, a mere 7 miles from the Scottish mainland. The total length of the causeways is just under 2 miles and 40,000 cubic metres of rock was topped off with 300,000 tonnes of concrete blocks. As the Geneva Convention forbade employment of prisoners of war on military schemes, the government was at pains to point out that, notwithstanding any defence imperitive, the barriers were intended for civilian purposes.

The Churchill Barriers and the road access they now provided from Orkney Mainland to Burray and South Ronaldsay were formally opened by the First Lord of the Admiralty in May 1945 just as the war was ending, their defensive purpose thankfully redundant. Today the Italian presence, and the friendly rapport struck up between them and Orcadians, is marked by the beautiful and moving Italian chapel constructed by those prisoners of war on Lamb Holm, adjacent to the first barrier.

POST-WAR TRENDS AND DEVELOPMENTS

In common with the rest of Scotland, and indeed the Western world, life in Orkney was transformed in the half century after the Second World War. Living standards of the archipelago's 20,000 or so people improved immeasurably, agriculture prospered and the pattern of transport was transformed. Two key trends drove the transport revolution. The first was the rapid development of air services and the second was the exponential boom in car ownership and road motor transport.

An invaluable legacy from the war was the construction of a hard topped aerodrome at Grimsetter near Kirkwall. This and other military airfields in the Highlands and Islands formed the key infrastructure for the development of post-war passenger air services.

Air services are not central to this story but to put them into perspective, it will be recalled that Captain Fresson pioneered commercial Orkney air services during the 1930s. A year or so after the War's end, the Labour government of the day nationalised Highland Airways and incorporated it into British European Airways (BEA). Under London control, inefficiencies mushroomed, costs rose, the service deteriorated and shamefully, Ted Fresson, who had done so much to develop air travel in the north, was frozen out and left BEA's employ in 1948. However, with cross subsidisation for the next 40 years the service provided by BEA's (later British Airways) linking

Kirkwall (Grimsetter) with Aberdeen, Inverness and the South (and also with Shetland) grew year on year as shown below:

Passengers by air to and from Kirkwall

1952	21,707
1960	33,139
1972	68,938
1994	89,000
2004	102,000

Of the southern airports of origin and destination, Aberdeen has always predominated, with Edinburgh also remaining important. This seems to reflect closely the traditional links established over the previous century by the North Co. These air services undeniably generated new business, but they also took passenger traffic from the North Co.'s sea link between Orkney and Aberdeen/Leith so that by the 1960s, the air service was handling over 90 per cent of the passenger traffic.

Meanwhile the near-universal adoption of the motor car gradually created a whole new market for shipping services that was to turn the pattern of trade on its head. As we know, Orkney's main southern links had hitherto been with Aberdeen and Leith. The *St Ola*'s Pentland Firth operation was regarded as a relatively minor branch operation. The war of course brought a massive increase in traffic across the Firth but after the cessation of hostilities it may have been expected that things would return to their pre-war pattern. This was not to be. With the opening of the Churchill Barriers, a bus service now provided five return trips per day between Kirkwall and St Margaret's Hope, with late runs on Saturday nights. This revolutionised the Hope's access to Kirkwall and its facilities. *St Ola*'s St Margaret's Hope call was no longer necessary and in any case, because of wartime restrictions, the Firth crossing between Stromness and Scrabster had been re-routed out of

Scapa Flow to west about Hoy. A distance of 28 miles, this is in fact the most direct route between the two ports, albeit exposed to the full force of westerly gales and Atlantic swells. In 1948 the old *St Ola* is recorded as having carried 286 cars, just under one per day – a sign of things to come – but the antiquated, much loved *St Ola* herself was old and due for scrapping.

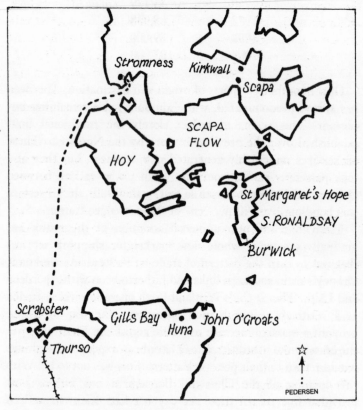

Fig. 5: The post-war Scrabster route

A new *St Ola* was ordered from Hall Russell's yard in Aberdeen and she came into service in 1951. A smart modern motor ship of 750 gross tons and 178 feet in length, *St Ola (II)* represented a much superior passenger experience and faster passage (two hours) compared with her predecessor. In her cargo space forward she could carry up to about 26 cars lifted on and off by derrick – a time-consuming process that on busy days took two and a half hours to load and two hours to discharge.

The old North Co. was taken over by Coast Lines in 1961 but the company name and style of service remained as before, although in the 20 years to the late 1960s, the number of cars carried had increased by over 20 times, to over 6,000 per year!

The summer peak demand became too much for *St Ola (II)* and from 1965 the North Co.'s cargo ship *St Clement* was brought in to supplement the peak carriage of vehicles. It is worth noting that passengers and cars accounted for 60 per cent of revenue, the mail contract 20 per cent, with the remaining 20 per cent coming from livestock and a small amount of mainly perishable cargo. The Pentland Firth traffic was, however, extremely seasonal and in 1968, 28 days were missed because of weather, mainly attributable to lack of shelter at Scrabster.

While the Pentland Firth traffic increased, air services had seriously eroded the Leith/Aberdeen services, to the extent that the passenger ship *St Magnus* was withdrawn in 1966 and replaced by a cargo ship. By 1968 only 3,422 passengers and 605 vehicles were carried on the long route, about 12 per cent and 10 per cent respectively of traffic on the Pentland Firth. The following diagrams at Fig. 6 illustrate the great difference in passenger carryings on the Pentland Firth Route (upper graph) and the Aberdeen/Leith Route (lower). The extreme summer peaks of traffic are clearly shown.

In terms of cargo tons, however, the Aberdeen/Leith route at that time still carried about seven and a half times that of the Pentland Firth route. By 1971 Leith was dropped as all long-distance services to Orkney and Shetland were concentrated on Aberdeen. From 1977 the Aberdeen services were reorganised as RO-RO (roll-on/roll-off) operations.

North Co. Passenger Carryings –1967
(Number of passengers)

Orkney
Pentland Firth route (ie Scrabster – Stromness only)

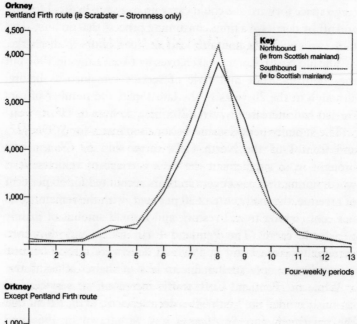

Orkney
Except Pentland Firth route

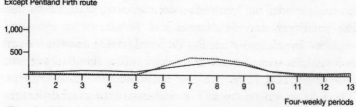

Fig. 6: The growing importance of the Scrabster route

5

ROLL-ON ROLL-OFF

For some time there had been disquiet about what were perceived as high levels of fares on the Orkney and Shetland services, and of course up until then the North Co.'s services operated on a purely commercial basis without government subsidy, other than mail contracts. The traditional lift-on/lift-off of handling cargo was time-consuming and expensive, but new ideas were emerging. The report of the Highland Transport Board in 1967 recognised the far-reaching changes that were taking place in the supply and demand for transport and they made a large number of radical proposals, including the replacement of several traditional shipping services by vehicle ferries operated on Norwegian principles. In the case of the Pentland Firth, the report opined:

'A vehicle ferry service across the Firth appears to be an operational possibility for the future. The Board recognise, however, that the idea has few attractions for the people of Orkney at the present time.' The report went on: 'If the shortest route across the Firth were chosen, a vehicle ferry could make two or three return trips a day, and given a reasonable load factor, this could keep sea transport costs down.' They recommended that: 'A Pentland Firth vehicle ferry crossing should be the subject of a comprehensive study.'

THE REPORT – 'A FERRY TO ORKNEY'

Since the opening of the Churchill Barriers and the direct road link they provided between Orkney Mainland and South

Ronaldsay, a short, frequent ferry crossing between Caithness and South Ronaldsay had seemed to offer real possibilities and had its advocates. A study was undertaken by the Highlands and Islands Development Board (HIDB) and the report, 'A Ferry to Orkney', was presented to the Secretary of State for Scotland in 1969. This document set out a wide range of opinions and estimated capital costs of various options for terminals.

Two main options were considered. These were on the one hand the established Stromness–Scrabster route, and on the other hand a shorter passage between South Ronaldsay and the nearest Caithness landfall passage. The National Farmers' Union, the Burray and South Ronaldsay District Council and Wick Town Council strongly supported a short crossing between South Ronaldsay and Gills Bay or John O'Groats. This option was demonstrated to give faster overall journey times. Strangely, there was no comparison made of relative operating costs, frequencies and fares as between the two options, which would undoubtedly have favoured the short South Ronaldsay route.

A key element of the report was evidence taken from experienced mariners including Trinity House pilot Captain Harry A. Banks that: 'A regular scheduled service could operate over the short sea route if the vessel had a speed of 15 knots.' Others as strongly supported a vehicle ferry on the existing Scrabster–Stromness route. The report concluded that: 'The "Small boat" men believe that the short crossing is perfectly safe and that the operators and masters of bigger vessels believe that the eastern Firth should be avoided.' The reporter failed to understand that the 'small boat' men were experienced in sailing *across* the Firth, i.e. the route of the short crossing, whereas the large vessel men would normally have sailed *through* the Firth, i.e. in an east–west direction, thereby encountering the worst of the tide races, over-falls, etc. It also ignored the fact that the route of the old *St Ola* and her predecessors had for over half a century crossed the Firth diagonally and passed over the Merry Men of Mey on a daily basis without mishap.

In the end, to the acute disappointment of the South Ronaldsay faction, the report came down on the side of Scrabster–Stromness as the route for a new vehicle ferry.

THE VEHICLE FERRY SERVICE

Notwithstanding overwhelming public scepticism of the idea of a vehicle ferry across the Firth, a new 15-knot RO-RO vehicle ferry with a capacity for 400 passengers and 90 cars was built and named *St Ola*, the third ferry so called. Delayed by contract slippage in completing required terminal works at Scrabster, *St Ola (III)* entered service in January 1975. In that year too Coast Lines was taken over by P&O Ferries and the traditional North of Scotland Orkney and Shetland Shipping Co. name ceased to be used. The following year the new ferry carried 15,000 vehicles and by 1991 vehicle traffic reached 30,000 cars and 6,500 commercial vehicles. By then, *St Ola (III)* was inadequate for her purpose and in 1992 a larger (but older, second-hand) replacement German-built ferry was acquired and again she was given the name *St Ola (IV)* – the fourth of the name on the route. This vessel had a capacity of 500 passengers and 120 cars. It is a matter of little speculation, how few, if any, of those who formerly opposed the RO-RO concept continued to do so once its practicality and convenience had been demonstrated. This goes to show that public opinion is often rooted in the past and can be slow to grasp the worth of new and more effective ideas.

Thus P&O Scottish Ferries continued with a variant of their customary pattern of service throughout the nineties in the form of three passenger/RO-RO services: Aberdeen–Lerwick direct, Aberdeen Lerwick via Stromness, and their daily return Pentland Firth crossing between Stromness and Scrabster. The long distance routes were augmented by a freight ferry. During the financial year 1995/6 a subsidy in the form of a block grant of £8.3 million was payable, of which £7.6 million went direct to

P&O. The remaining £700,000 for livestock shipments was shared between P&O and freight operator Orcargo. Change was in the air, however. In 1995, in response to the requirements of European law, the Scottish Office announced that in future subsidies for shipping services would have to go out to tender.

By early 1997 a contract for the three Northern Isles routes was put out to tender. In May a general election brought in a new Labour government, and with this came the possibility that state-owned Caledonian MacBrayne would be included in the tender process. Under the previous Conservative administration's scheme the tender process had been open only to the private sector, so CalMac had hitherto been excluded. In the event, P&O were awarded a five-year contract covered by an annual block grant of £11 million with a claw-back clause should profits exceed forecasts, but incredibly with no constraint on the rates they charged. This five-year contract was, however, presented as a holding operation pending a new tender to operate from 2002 that would follow a re-evaluation of Northern Isles services. For the meantime the new arrangement enabled P&O to see the millennium out.

By 2000 traffic on the Stromness–Scrabster route reached 157,800 passengers and 47,100 cars. This was the high point that would not be achieved again by P&O. It is instructive to note by comparison that in 2000, the Aberdeen–Orkney direct RO-RO service carried a mere 20,300 passengers and 3,100 cars. Notwithstanding the £11 million subsidy, the whole issue of ferries to and from Orkney was about to go into the melting pot! But first we need to go back almost three decades to revisit how the short sea route and its supporters developed their ideas.

6

THE SHORT SEA CROSSING

Although by the early 1970s officialdom had decided to back longer, more expensive and less frequent Scrabster–Stromness passage as the new Orkney vehicle ferry route, the short sea crossing of the Pentland Firth was too good an idea to let lapse.

PASSENGER SERVICES

In 1972, after half a decade of discussion and scheming about the short sea route, Captain William (Bill) Banks of St Margaret's Hope acquired a 75-foot converted air–sea rescue launch which he named *Pentalina*. Bill Banks was Andrew Banks' uncle, and brother of Captain Harry Banks of Trinity House, who had some years earlier suggested that the short sea crossing was a feasible proposition. The launch was modified on the Tyne to make her suitable for passenger service and she arrived at St Margaret's Hope in March. Captain Banks had intended to start operating between the Hope and John O'Groats immediately, but the pier at John O'Groats was inadequate. It was not until he had installed a floating pontoon at the Caithness port that the service started late in May. Thereafter *Pentalina* ran two return trips daily with a connecting bus to and from Kirkwall. The departure times from St Margaret's Hope were 07:45 and 17:30, with corresponding return departures from John O'Groats at 09:30 and 19:00. For the first time it was possible for day return trips to be made in either direction, allowing patrons a significant time ashore at either end.

For a few weeks a return sailing was provided to Hoy on

Thursdays but this was discontinued, due presumably to lack of patronage. The main Pentland Firth operation ran until the second last weekend of September and it is recorded that some 12,000 passengers were carried that first season, of which 90 per cent originated from the southern port. *Pentalina* ran on the route for one more summer but the operation was not continued thereafter and Bill Banks turned his attention to more lucrative business opportunities. These opportunities mainly took the form of Flotta Marine, a company that handled supplies and workforce transport to and from the construction site on the nearby island of Flotta, which was at that time being developed as a major oil trans-shipment terminal.

The next attempt at a short sea crossing was to take root. Two local businessmen, Ian Thomas and Donnie Bews, after experimenting with a fast sea taxi, *Pentland Atom*, made a business decision to start a summer passenger ferry on the traditional route between John O'Groats, where the Caithness County Council had undertaken pier improvements, and Burwick, the most southerly port on South Ronaldsay. This scheme, therefore, took advantage of the shortest feasible crossing between Caithness and Orkney. In 1976 they bought a small passenger vessel, *Souters Lass*, which had previously been run by Fred Newton, a Ross-shire bus operator, to carry workers between Cromarty and Nigg in connection with the oilrig fabrication yard that had recently been established there. This service, which is still operational and marketed under the name John O'Groats Ferry, was a success and in 1987 *Souters Lass* was sold to run cruises from Fort William, and a new vessel, *Pentland Venture*, was purpose-built for the route. She still operates from 1 May to 30 September each year, with coach connections in Orkney to/from Kirkwall via the Churchill Barriers and on the southern leg between John O'Groats and Inverness. The through journey between Kirkwall and Inverness takes just 4 hours 40 minutes. Day tours of Orkney are also offered. *Pentland Venture* was later lengthened and can now carry up to 250 passengers. Two return trips daily are offered in May and September and four return trips daily in June, July and August on the 40-minute crossing.

The John O'Groats Ferry has become an important contributor to Orkney tourism but it does not convey vehicles other than bicycles, and it is seasonal. John O'Groats is too exposed for all-year operation and too restricted to handle a vehicle ferry. The ideal potential port for a vehicle ferry operation was still thought to be Gills Bay, about four miles to the west.

During the 1980s, the local community at Gills Bay backed an initiative by the harbour committee to stabilise and enhance the old pier. Rock-dredging and strengthening were carried out and a new south pier built under a 'Job Creation' scheme. It was in 1987 that the concept of a year-round vehicle ferry for the short sea crossing based on Gills Bay was to re-emerge as a serious business proposition. In response, Highland Regional Council were persuaded to zone Gills Harbour for transport activity in its Local and Structure Plans and to provide a modern-standard 6-metre-wide access road.

The principals behind the new venture were Ken Cadenhead and John Rose of Argyll-based Western Ferries, of which more later, together with Orkney businessmen Jim Peace and Alfie Banks (father of Andrew Banks), and they formed a new company which they called Orkney Ferries. Their plan was to run a vehicle ferry service every two hours from Gills Bay in Caithness to the nearest Orkney landfall of Burwick. Of course Burwick, with its physical road connection to Orkney Mainland via the Churchill Barriers, is only 17 miles from Kirkwall. One of Alfie Banks' motivations was to create an economical means of getting fish from his son's salmon farm to the Scottish mainland because at that time the only option was P&O Ferries, on which the charge for an artic (articulated truck) was £1,200.

There was a groundswell of support for the plan within the Highland Regional Council but there was also scepticism by

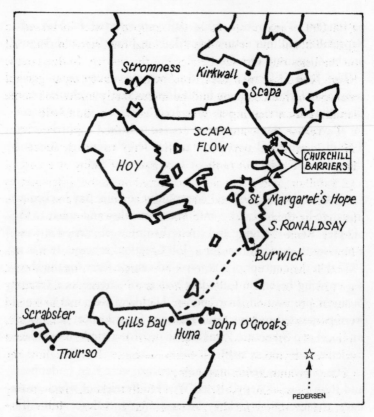

Fig. 7: The planned Orkney Ferries short sea crossing of 1989

some Orkney councillors, particularly those who were thirled to
the Scrabster–Stromness service. Nevertheless Orkney Islands
Council (OIC) as a whole was supportive of the plan and
approved planning consent for the terminal at Burwick, agree-
ing to use its Oil Fund to finance construction of the terminals
at both Burwick and Gills Bay. The Oil Fund had been created
for the benefit of the Orkney population from a throughput levy
on each barrel of oil that passed through the Flotta terminal,
and was regarded as private money. The cost estimate for the
works was just under £2 million. OIC also agreed to take

£100,000 worth of shares in the company (later increased to £200,000) and to put suitable directional road signs in place, all on the basis that Orkney Ferries ran the service. In due course South Ronaldsay man Ken Brookman was taken on as general manager of the company and he immediately undertook some familiarisation training at Western Ferries on the Clyde.

To realise this concept, of course, required a purpose-built ship. John Rose arranged for the ship to be designed by Harrisons Clyde and built by Cochranes of Selby at a cost of £2.5 million, and a fine ship she turned out to be. Fifty metres long, she was designed to carry 150 passengers, 50 cars, or up to five commercial vehicles. A children's competition was held to find a name for the new ship and the winning entry was *Varagen*, which in Old Norse means 'our own'. She was formally named by Lisa Tullock at a ceremony after the vessel arrived at Scapa in July 1989. The name *Varagen* should strictly speaking be pronounced 'Var*age*n' with the stress on the second syllable, as in modern Norwegian *vår egen*, but in Orkney it is universally pronounced '*Var*agen' with the stress on the first syllable – etymologically off beam no doubt, but somehow the Orkney pronunciation has a ring to it.

Varagen was the first British ferry built to the then new safety regulations following the Zebrugge ferry disaster. John Rose also arranged for the design and installation of the berthing and vehicle handling facilities at the two ports. At Burwick a breakwater was built, the harbour dredged, a vehicle marshalling area cleared. Then the terminal was fitted with a link-span, or hinged bridge, designed to link the ship with the shore so that vehicles could drive on and off at any state of the tide.

Unfortunately the terminal installation at Gills Bay was less satisfactory – disastrously so! Originally a breakwater was to have been constructed at Gills to provide shelter at this relatively exposed site but, as the costs were by that stage well over budget (by £3 million), OIC were unable, or unwilling, to commit any further funds. At this point OIC took over the terminals and announced that the agreement between the council and Orkney Ferries was void. It was now up to Orkney Ferries to complete the works at Gills Bay as best they could. Some dredging was carried out and a link-span put in place. To align the ship with the link-span, two dolphins (large vertical cylinders set into the sea bed) were placed some 6 metres to the east of the centre line of vessel and link-span. Thus, as the ship lay against these, she was perfectly positioned to engage with the link-span. Critically, however, there was no protection from swell.

With the arrival of *Varagen* from the builders, a number of trial trips were arranged between the two as yet incomplete terminals. These trials revealed the first problem at both terminals with the grounding of *Varagen* at low tides, indicating a need for further dredging. Then Captain Cameron resigned, as he believed berthing at Gills Bay in a swell without a breakwater to be too risky. Pending remedial work, an interim service commenced in mid August between Gills Bay and Houton on Orkney Mainland, but the service was plagued by breakdowns and uncertainties and restricted to 12 passengers, as the Department of Trade and Industry would not issue a passenger certificate until the Gills Bay terminal was shown to be practicable. Runs were made intermittently. Then on the evening of 16 September, a westerly gale lifted the link-span off its seating (hinge) with such force that it broke adrift.

That was it for the Orkney Ferries short sea crossing. *Varagen* was laid up in Grangemouth and the crews paid off. Although OIC had agreed to spend a further £3.3 million on the project, they never did. Support within the council for the short sea crossing had never been unanimous and the link-span problem gave new force to the naysayers' arguments. OIC had lost confidence in the project. With what seems undue haste, the council arranged for a lorry to pick up signs and buoys and the compressors used to operate the link-spans, thereby rendering the service inoperable. The terminals were left in an incomplete state and in the circumstances the company was forced into liquidation, the directors losing their investment.

It was a tragedy that the Gills Bay–Burwick service was so close to fruition but was killed off before it had been able to prove its potential. For all that, its impact was significant. OIC inherited the excellent *Varagen*, which thereafter supplemented the *Earl Sigurd* and *Earl Thorfinn* on the council-operated Kirkwall to North Isles service, and in that capacity she has always been regarded as much the superior vessel of the trio. The name Orkney Ferries was also henceforth transferred to the OIC's own North and South Isles ferry operation. The threat of the short sea crossing shook P&O Ferries out of their comfortable monopolistic complacency. Since its inception, the Stromness–Scrabster service had operated on the basis of one return trip per day. Two return sailings were provided for the first time and then in 1992 a larger replacement *St Ola* was put in service on this more frequent basis.

AFTERMATH

The first battle for a short vehicle ferry crossing of the Pentland Firth may have been lost for now, but the war was still to be won. Meantime the example of Orkney Ferries in challenging P&O was an inspiration to another Orkney-based businessman – David Laidlaw. He founded Orcargo to operate a RO–RO cargo and livestock service between Kirkwall and Invergordon with his ex-Falkland Islands ship *Contender*. This excellent service started in March 1992 and had the effect of encouraging P&O to slash their previously overpriced commercial vehicle rates dramatically. Orcargo ran for eight years, only to succumb to bankruptcy in 1999, due to what was widely believed to be predatory pricing by the heavily subsidised P&O. The government had withdrawn freight subsidy and in its place announced that all state funding would go henceforth to P&O as a 'passenger lifeline' subsidy. P&O then simply used its 'passenger' subsidy to discount its freight rates to secure most of Orcargo's freight business. This was a finding of the Westminster Scottish Affairs Select Committee Report on the Withdrawal of Tariff Rebate Subsidy in 1997. Orcargo continued to be run by the administrator until July 2000, when it was taken over by freight operator Streamline and the *Contender* struggled on until April 2001, when she sailed for the last time.

Meanwhile the community-owned Gills Bay Harbour Association had commissioned a number of reports and the Association's secretary, John Ross, had hand-recorded tide, wave and wind-speed data for over a year before an electronic system was installed. So accurate and useful were these records that later analysis and detailed calibration of these tidal data by the Bidston Tidal laboratory on Merseyside revealed a hitherto unknown phenomenon of tidal surges in the area. Peter Iles of the major transport consultancy, MDS Transmodal of Chester, analysed the data, and carried out further detailed assessments of the port to conclude that the 'short crossing from Gills Bay offered an absolute advantage over other routes to and from Orkney and represented a superior product to all concerned' (Gills Bay Harbour Study, January 1993).

Despite the Orkney Ferries debacle, from which hard lessons had been learned, the Gills Bay interests were approached a few years later by Andrew Banks, who had set up a new company, Pentland Ferries Ltd, and a partnership arrangement was struck between harbour association and operator to develop a vehicle ferry service on the short sea route from Gills Bay.

7

ANDREW BANKS ENTERS
THE ARENA

Andrew Alfred Banks comes from a long line of Orkney farmers, boat builders and seafarers, including sailing ship masters. He was born in Kirkwall, son of Andrew Alfred (Alfie) Banks of Smiddybanks Farm, St Margaret's Hope, on South Ronaldsay and Sarah (Sally) Jean Norquoy. Alfie's brothers, Captains Harry and Bill Banks, had been interested in the short sea crossing, as described in the previous chapter. Andrew's formal schooling at St Margaret's Hope and Kirkwall was enhanced by practical life on the farm and going creeling for lobsters in his own little dingy. This youthful experience laid a strong foundation of self-reliance, staying-power and an innate ability to tackle and solve problems from first principles – characteristics that were to prove their worth time and again as our story unfolds.

ANDREW BANKS'S EARLY CAREER

When he left school, Andrew started work with his uncle's company, Flotta Marine Services. This was at the time when the exploitation of Scotland's North Sea oil was coming on-stream. The main impact of this on Orkney was the development of an oil trans-shipment terminal on the small island of Flotta which lies to the west of St Margaret's Hope. Its purpose was and is reception and discharge of tankers from North Sea oil fields and the loading of other tankers bound for the major oil refining ports such as Rotterdam or the Gulf. These tankers are massive ships. Working on crew boats, small tugs moving tankers, further developed Andrew's seamanship skills.

On 3 May 1986 Andrew married Susan Henderson, daughter of Jimmy and May Henderson from Leith, and the couple set up home in St Margaret's Hope. After five or six years with Orkney Marine Services, Andrew moved into salmon and oyster farming with funding from his father, Orkney Islands Council and Highlands and Islands Development Board. Once this operation was up and running, he was joined by his brother. In the 1980s, fish farming was seen as a major opportunity for coastal communities and indeed there were some good years. There were also bad years; in particular 1992, when prices collapsed due to Norwegian salmon flooding the market. The fish farming enterprise was no longer as attractive as it had been and Andrew wanted out. A few years later he took the opportunity to sell the fish farming business.

The idea of the short sea crossing had lain dormant since 1989 but was by no means forgotten by the Banks family. The disposal of the salmon farming business presented a fresh chance for the next generation to resuscitate the project. Andrew said to his father, 'I'm keen to have a go at the short sea crossing. What do you think?' Alfie, who had more reason than most to be wary of revisiting the venture, responded, 'Well if you can find a suitable ship, I'll help with the finance.' That was in 1997, the start of what was eventually going to be one of the most remarkable and hard-fought accomplishments in modern Scottish maritime development. That same year Pentland Ferries was incorporated.

FINDING A SHIP

As a first step, Andrew contacted the Liverpool shipbrokers S C Chambers to ascertain if any passenger/RO-RO ferries were on the market. One month later, Chalmers communicated that the Caledonian MacBrayne (CalMac) ferry *Pioneer* was for sale and general arrangement drawings were sent to Orkney post haste. Andrew then got in touch with the firm of naval architects, Strathclyde Maritime Design, met their representative and went for a trip on *Pioneer* to assess her suitability for the Pentland Firth. The price was reasonable at £100,000, and her shallow draft was a useful attribute, but her vehicle capacity was limited to 30 cars loaded over the stern only. Indeed, about half of the main (vehicle) deck was taken up by passenger accommodation – a singularly inefficient arrangement for a vehicle ferry. He considered reconfiguring the main deck and fitting a bow door, but ultimately dismissed this as impracticable.

In the meantime, Andrew passed through Troon, where another time-served CalMac ferry, *Iona*, was in the wet berth. But *Iona* seemed too big and was in any case not at that point on the market. She was, however, a well-designed 'roll through' vehicle ferry, with bow and stern loading, and the entire main deck available for carrying 47 cars, or equivalent commercial vehicles. Then in October 1997, Andrew found that Caledonian MacBrayne had changed their mind, and wished to keep the *Pioneer* but dispose of the *Iona*. The stated price was £350,000 but CalMac's chairman, Sandy Ferguson, indicated that he was keen to get the ship off their books and would sell if offered £250,000 cash. And so a deal was struck. Andrew Banks was now the owner of a vehicle ferry and poised to start operations on the short sea crossing once the terminals were brought up to standard. That, as would become apparent, was easier said than done.

BUREAUCRATIC CAT AND MOUSE

It was only natural to assume that Orkney Islands Council (OIC) would be impressed with this initiative by a native son, but that was in fact far from the case. The name *Pentalina* traditionally used by the Banks family was not at the time available so *Iona* was renamed *Pentalina B* and she sailed north to arrive at St

Margaret's Hope on 26 October. Councillors and council officials were invited to inspect the vessel at her new home port. The council's attitude became clear on the occasion of the visit by the look of horror on the face of key officials when Andrew proudly announced that he had bought the ship and intended to start operating the short sea route.

The council's negative, and now obstructive, attitude was confirmed when access to Gills Bay Harbour was sought. Since the time of the original Orkney Ferries project Orkney Islands Council had taken a 99-year lease from Gills Bay Harbour Committee on the former terminal area at Gills Bay, and when Andrew Banks tried to negotiate a sub-lease, OIC refused to cooperate. To prevail over this blatant attempt by the council to block the project, Andrew commissioned Strathclyde Maritime Design to prepare a layout for a link-span to be built on an alternative part of the Gills Harbour land, beyond the area covered by the OIC lease. When this layout had been completed and was at the stage of being approved by Gills Bay Harbour Committee, OIC signalled that they were after all prepared to assign the lease to Andrew Banks. The council's spoiling tactic had delayed the start of work by two months and caused unnecessary expenditure.

Much work was required to develop the Gills Bay terminal so that it could receive a vehicle ferry service with some degree of reliability. Andrew estimated this would cost £900,000, far less than the £5 million previously estimated by Orkney Islands Council. To fund the reconstruction of the Gills Bay terminal, Andrew applied to OIC for a commercial loan of £300,000 with the ship as security, but this was refused. This caused a financial domino effect. As the council had turned down the loan, the local development agency, Orkney Enterprise, also felt obliged to back down, as did the local branches of the Royal Bank of Scotland and the Clydesdale Bank. It was as though a local mafia of vested interests had ganged up against the new venture for reasons which are still not completely clear. It was the Bank of

Scotland that came to the rescue. The local manager indicated that the issue was 'too political' for him but helpfully arranged for the Inverness manager to visit and arrange the loan.

Andrew also needed the OIC-owned Burwick ferry terminal to be upgraded but the council refused to do this, so Andrew indicated that he was prepared to rent the terminal and undertake the necessary work himself. This offer was also declined. Andrew had therefore no alternative but to select the independently owned and sympathetic St Margaret's Hope as his Orkney landfall. This would result in a longer route, but still much shorter and more sheltered than Scrabster–Stromness.

At this time, Andrew applied to Highlands and Islands Enterprise for assistance, but after a 'detailed analysis' they decided against supporting the project – the reasons given were concerns about the choice of Gills Bay as the Caithness terminal; doubts over the suitability of the vessel; the effect on other operators; and lack of political support, particularly on the part of OIC, and now additionally, it seemed, from the Scottish Office. Discussion with Edinburgh civil servants revealed an apparent antipathy towards the project and a sense that 'the short sea route had been tried before and it didn't work'. As far as they were concerned, it seemed, the only game in town was Stromness–Scrabster.

In April 1998, before work on the terminals started, word came from Caledonian MacBrayne that their large Stornoway–Ullapool ferry *Isle of Lewis* had suffered a major mechanical fault and had to be withdrawn for repair. The Mull ferry *Isle of Mull* was moved to the Stornoway station and the otherwise idle *Pentalina B* was hastily chartered back by CalMac to fill the gap for several weeks on the Mull run. This provided an unexpected and useful income stream to Pentland Ferries. Meantime, using funds from the sale of the fish farm and his father's contribution, Andrew made a start on creating a terminal at Gills Bay to which *Pentalina B* could operate.

STARTING WORK AT GILLS BAY TERMINAL

All that existed at Gills Bay in 1998 was a small boat harbour, the two dolphins and the marshalling area, which lay too low above high water, part of the reason the original link-span had been washed away. The first, preparatory, phase of the plan was to tidy up the site and open up the rock armour at the nose of the pier under the former link-span, then to move that rock armour to the west to form the beginnings of a breakwater and to dredge and form a relocated vessel berthing and manoeuvring area. Two options presented themselves to Andrew Banks: engage an outside contractor (expensive); or do the work himself. Being the man he is, there was no contest – he'd do it himself!

In April 1999 *Pentalina B* was taken to Lerwick for dry-docking and refitting and during the summer she had her cumbersome hoist removed, as it would be unnecessary for operating the short sea route.

First action to initiate construction work was to attend a plant auction in Errol near Dundee, where he bought a dump truck and excavator/digger; he took these, with the JCB and crane he already had, to the site, along with a caravan. Andrew and three other workers – Jocky Rosie, Stevie Gutcher and Jimmy Simison – planned to live on site for the duration, though only two of the workers would be on the workforce at any one time.

They made a start tidying up the site, but it was September 1999 before Highland Council unanimously endorsed the plans for the terminal. The initial major work involved creating a breakwater by moving existing rock armour from its former position with the excavator and crane. Then the existing concrete bank seat (link-span hinge) had to be broken up, and a trench dug into the seabed to bed rock, so that in due course a new link-span could be located in a more sheltered position, some 25 metres to landward but on the same alignment as the old one. With the trench dug out, more rock armour was moved from the east of the harbour to the west and deposited seawards towards the first dolphin.

Progress was set back by a force-ten storm; the site and caravan flooded, and electric power shorted out at midnight. A local fishing boat broke free of its moorings and was being pounded against rocks. Efforts to save the boat took most of the night; with no sleep, soaked through and exhausted, the bedraggled team saw the storm abate by morning and the whole harbour area strewn with tangles of seaweed.

That first year progress was slow, because of sporadic gales throughout the winter of 1999–2000. By spring of 2000, however, shuttering had been put in place on both sides of the landward end of the trench to create a concrete box with walls up to 3 metres thick, within which the link-span would be located. The eastern edge was tied into the existing pier and the parallel western edge aligned with the existing dolphins.

Meantime dredging proceeded. The technique was to build a temporary bund or roadway down the beach so that the digger could dig out the boulder clay on the ferry berth side and dump it for removal on the other side. Boulder clay, as its name describes, is like a pudding of clay generously laced with boulders – a glacial deposit from the end of the last Ice Age. These boulders can be troublesome. The biggest found in the Gills Bay project was somewhere between 12 and 15 tons! Feeling underwater, Andrew managed to get it curled into the digger's bucket and as it was extracted it was the full height of the digger arm, measuring nearly 4 metres long by about 1 metre in diameter. As the 65-ton Akerman digger lifted this massive stone off the sea bed and swung it round to the other side of the harbour the machine was just on its tipping point. But the manoeuvre was completed without mishap. The rock lay there. Leslie Ross, using the small digger, tried to move it but to no avail. Then a couple of months later it simply split in half of its own accord. Isn't nature wonderful!

Other dramas interrupted the smooth flow of work too. One

day the digger burst a hydraulic pipe while digging out a channel, necessitating an immediate trip to Wick (about 18 miles away) to get a replacement. In the meantime the tide turned so Andrew had to put on his dry-suit and go into the rapidly rising sea to remove the faulty pipe, then re-enter the water when the replacement pipe arrived, holding his breath as he struggled to refit the hydraulic pipe underwater. There was a twist in the pipe and it was difficult to get the other end in place. He managed to get one bolt secured but was beaten by the rising tide and had to abandon the effort. This meant that the digger had no hydraulic fluid. Billy McGee, the Gills Bay rope man, came to the rescue by bringing his yawl alongside, and topping up the hydraulic fluid from it. Andrew and Leslie miraculously managed to start the digger, turned it through 180 degrees only to be thwarted again when the next wave flooded the electrics. The digger had to be abandoned for that day as Billy came back with his yawl to take Andrew and Leslie ashore.

At low water early next morning, the bulldozer and dumper were positioned down the beach to drag the digger back to dry land but with the dead weight of its tracks, it would not budge. Again the attempt had to be abandoned. Later that day, at high water, a local lobster fisherman laying creels just offshore couldn't understand why a digger jib was sticking out of the water! On the next low tide, late that afternoon, with the aid of a portable hydraulic pump and by releasing the digger's brakes, the dumper managed to tow the digger to safety ashore. Within two days the much-needed digger was going again. It kept going for another eight years!

EXTENDING GILLS PIER

On completion of the dredging, work began on the main element of the terminal: building a new protective wharf or pier for the *Pentalina B* to lie alongside when engaged with the link-span. This was intended to right a major flaw of the original scheme – lack of shelter, particularly from the west. The objective was to fill in the space between the link-span 'box' and the first dolphin with a steel framework faced with piles and backfilled, then to repeat the process between the two dolphins. This would create a solid wall which would protect both the ferry vessel and the link-span from swell and wind.

Andrew Banks had never before attempted piling but, undaunted, purchased the necessary equipment, this time returning from another trip to Errol at night in thick driving snow – a marathon run with his sore eyes feeling, he later described, 'as though they were standing out on stalks'. A series of three 'H' beams were butt-welded end to end to form a single 30-metre (100-foot) beam to be stretched between shore and dolphin, one at high-water level and low-water level. These long beams formed the framework for the piles. By an ingenious method of supporting one end of the beam on terra firma at the landward end, with the seaward end resting on a steel boat purchased for this purpose, the crane swung and then lowered the whole assembly into position. It took but two days to get the high and low beams into position. Then the process of driving piles commenced – some 25 piles to the east and a similar number to the west. Inevitably, halfway to the first dolphin a storm blew up. The piles waggled but held – whew! After the storm abated, the line of piles to the first dolphin could be completed. The team then filled the cavity between the two lines of piles with spoil and backfilled on the exposed western side. The beams and piles procedure was then repeated between the first and second dolphins. The new pier was now in place and focus shifted to installation of the link-span.

Andrew and two welders set to construction of a suitable link-span on the shore at St Margaret's Hope – a considerable feat, bearing in mind the limited facilities available. Once it was assembled, a trench was dug into the shore and *Pentalina B* was backed into it and the link-span eased onto the ship's vehicle deck. *Pentalina B* took the link-span across to Gills Bay, after which it took a few further weeks to complete the steel support structure, control mechanism and power pack installation for raising and lowering the link-span. Of course, Andrew himself plumbed in the hydraulic pipe work. The link-span was lifted into place and passed the requisite tests with flying colours.

One final essential job was to raise and concrete the whole marshalling area by 1 metre so that it would be well clear of the highest tidal surges, and at last the Gills Bay terminal was in operational condition.

WORKS AT ST MARGARET'S HOPE

The principle behind the short sea crossing is to minimise the passage distance between island and mainland terminals, thereby enabling more round trips in the day, maximising the traffic carrying capacity of the route and minimising unit costs to operator and customers. Almost without exception, short sea crossings have encouraged new traffic when they have been introduced elsewhere, bringing substantial economic and social benefits to the local communities.

The best option for reducing the passage distance on the Pentland Firth is, as already discussed, to operate between Gills Bay and Burwick, the nearest Orkney port. While the independent Gills Bay Harbour Committee was wholly supportive of the Pentland Ferries plan, the same was by no means the case with Orkney Islands Council who controlled Burwick. The OIC indicated very clearly that they had no plans to bring the facilities there up to the specification required to receive a vehicle ferry. Indeed there remained a sense that the project, like the first Orkney Ferries attempt, was unlikely to succeed and that it was not worth putting more good money after bad. As a result, Andrew Banks decided, for the immediate future at least, to make St Margaret's Hope his Orkney terminal. The advantage of the Hope was that it was under the control of a local harbour trust which, like Gills Bay, was supportive of the plan for a short sea crossing. The Hope is also a very sheltered harbour. The down side of St Margaret's Hope is that the passage from there to Gills Bay is longer – a little more than an hour at *Pentalina B*'s cruising speed, compared with half an hour in the case of Burwick. Even though this meant fewer crossings per day would be possible, the Hope–Gills Bay option still offered shorter and more frequent vehicle ferry services than any other then available.

With work on the Gills Bay terminal well advanced, Andrew's team made a start turning the Hope into a vehicle ferry terminal. A good pier has existed there since 1906 and no major work was required in that regard, but a link-span had to be installed. More ingenuity. Two short link-spans formerly used by Shetland Island Council ferries and now surplus to requirements were purchased. These were brought to St Margaret's Hope and, on land adjacent to the pier, the two sections were butt-welded end to end to create a 30-metre length. A flotation tank was constructed and attached to support the seaward end. Meanwhile, local contractor Davie Taylor was brought in to construct the bank seat (land-side hinge) and marshalling area. Once the Hope link-span was in place the second terminal was ready for operation.

PREPARATIONS TO START THE SERVICE

By March 2001, with the terminals in place and *Pentalina B* now upgraded to the full satisfaction of the Maritime and Coastguard Agency (MCA), the *Orcadian* was able to report:

'South Ronaldsay businessman Andrew Banks announced that his short sea RO-RO ferry service would be open for business at the beginning of May. He had previously asked the council for financial support but his application was rejected on the grounds that a similar project in the late 1980s had ended in failure. Mr Banks said he had not had much help at all but was delighted that everything had worked out even though it had been a "long haul".'

Some polite understatements there! The facts were, however, essentially correct. A May start was indeed planned and towards the end of March advertisements were placed for experienced officers and seamen to work for Pentland Ferries – two shifts of 13 to operate three round trips a day from St Margaret's Hope to Gills Bay.

All that remained was to take *Pentalina B* for her survey and annual overhaul. In April Andrew, his wife and children sailed north with the ship to Lerwick for dry-docking and overhaul at Malakoff and Moore's dry-dock at Holmsgarth in Lerwick. The weather was foul, with snow and storm-force blizzards. The dry-dock was of the pontoon (or floating) dock type – basically a large flat barge with high sides and open ends. The dock can be temporarily sunk by controlled ingress of water to allow the vessel that is to be overhauled to be floated in through one end and between the sides. The whole structure is then raised by forcing the water out of the dock, thereby leaving the vessel high and dry and sitting on chocks (balks of timber). On this occasion, as the floating dock was raised, Andrew noticed that the wooden chocks supporting the ship were coming adrift due to the flexing of the dock in the swell, which meant that Andrew and the dock team had to stay up all night to tighten wedges as they came loose. As the overhaul progressed, Malakoff and Moore's foreman, Norman Moncrieff, and Andrew became friends and Norman mentioned that the company was considering selling the floating dock. The family spent that wild week in a chalet in Lerwick and rolled their Easter eggs in the snow and, with the overhaul successfully completed, it was a real relief to get home to St Margaret's Hope.

It had taken three gruelling years from starting negotiations at Gills Bay to the point at which the service was ready to commence.

8

THE NEW SERVICE STARTS

On Thursday, 3 May 2001, on Andrew's and Susan's fifteenth wedding anniversary, as planned, and without undue fuss, *Pentalina B* set off on her maiden voyage on the short sea RO-RO service from St Margaret's Hope to Gills Bay. She sailed under the command of Captain Kenny Bruce, who had come out of retirement especially to see *Pentalina B* and the new enterprise through its first week. Passengers on the maiden voyage enjoyed a smooth crossing in perfect weather conditions. Twelve passengers and five cars boarded at St Margaret's Hope for the one-hour journey to Gills Bay in Caithness, where Andrew's Uncle Bill, the short sea crossing pioneer, was first to drive off. Several more passengers and a lorry belonging to Caithness haulier John Cormack joined the ship for the return journey. According to press reports covering the event, passengers welcomed the new service, praising 'the short travelling time and convenient timetabling of the service', which was of course what the whole concept was about.

The ship was restricted to 12 passengers until a passenger certificate could be issued – cargo vessels are permitted to carry up to 12 passengers without such a certificate. On the second week, Captain Robbie Drever took over as master of *Pentalina B*. He had been skipper with the former Orkney coastal shipping company Dennison Shipping. Captain Drever had to be tested for a pilot exemption certificate to allow him to command a vessel carrying more than 12 passengers in these waters, and this was held up because the examining officer was on holiday. Once this hurdle had been cleared, a Class VI certificate to permit

Pentalina B to carry 250 passengers in summer and 49 cars was duly awarded. In presenting this important document, the issuing officer from the MCA warned ominously, 'I can't stop you operating, but make one mistake and we'll close you down.' It was hinted (outrageously) that 'certain civil servants in the Scottish Executive' had sought to prevent the operation from starting. No explanation was given. Fortunately, there were no mistakes.

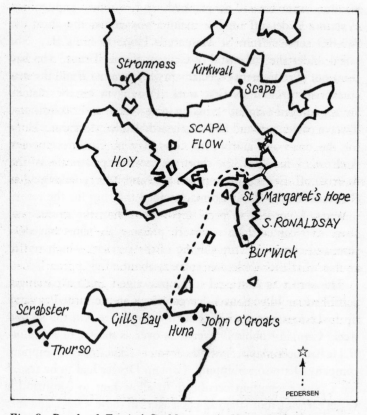

Fig. 8: Pentland Ferries' St Margaret's Hope–Gills Bay route

Andrew Banks was now able to announce that he was 'prepared to take on the heavyweights'. Three round trips per day were scheduled, leaving St Margaret's Hope at 08:00, 12:00 and 17:00 with return departures from Gills Bay at 09:45, 13:45 and 18:45. For the first time ever this allowed Orcadians to take their car or van to the Scottish mainland on any day of the week for either four or eight hours and get home again that night – a previously unheard-of provision and immeasurably superior to P&O Ferries' two-hour journey time between Scrabster and Stromness with two return trips, timed so as to afford no time at all ashore for Orcadians visiting the Scottish mainland and wishing to return the same day.

The fare structure was a refreshingly simple flat rate one-way charge of £10.00 per passenger and £25.00 per car. This compared with P&O Ferries' standard single on the Scrabster–Stromness route of £16.50 for a passenger and £51.00 for a car. In short, travel on Pentland Ferries was accomplished in nearly half the time, one and a half times more frequently, and for significantly less than half the price, exactly as advocates of the short sea crossing had maintained for years. It is no wonder that Orcadians flocked to the new route.

Within a month or so of certification the new service was often carrying a very creditable, almost unbelievable, 500 passengers and 150 cars per day. Because of the high traffic levels a marshalling lane had to be created on the approach road to the pier at St Margaret's Hope to avoid gridlock. Figures published for July showed that carryings on the three Pentland Firth services were as follows:

Pentland Firth Passengers – July 2001

Route	Operator	Passengers
John O'Groats–Burwick	John O'Groats Ferry	10,893
Gills Bay–St Margaret's Hope	Pentand Ferries	11,621
Scrabster–Stromness	P&O Ferries	18,554

Bearing in mind that there had been no pre-advertising, 'just in case', this result vindicated the short sea route. Seventy thousand brochures had been hurriedly printed and they had all disappeared by the end of the season. In the first year little freight was carried as the hauliers were understandably concerned about reliability. By the end of the first summer, to the delight of Andrew and his family, Pentland Ferries had taken in about £1 million in revenue.

The star of the show, *Pentalina B* herself, justified Andrew's hopes and proved to be a particularly steady sea boat ideally suited to the quirky Pentland Firth. She was built in 1970 by Ailsa of Troon as *Iona* for David MacBrayne as their first and only 'roll through' vehicle ferry, before that venerable company was overtaken by the formation of Caledonian MacBrayne. Originally intended for the Islay route, her first station was between Gourock and Dunoon on the Clyde. She inaugurated RO-RO operation to Stornoway, firstly from Kyle of Lochalsh and then from Ullapool, subsequently to serve on virtually every CalMac route prior to her sale to Pentland Ferries. The promenade deck had broad alleyways on each side, with an open circulating area aft. There was a covered observation lounge forward with comfortable seating. Between the alleyways amidships were the lobby, purser's office, luggage space and toilets. Further aft was the cosy dining saloon where, such is the friendly informality of the space, the latest gossip could be exchanged or business deals set in motion over a cup of tea or a meal. The upper deck, which has featured more than once on television, offered a good all round view of the ever-changing and fascinating scene that the hour-long passage presents.

Operating from St Margaret's Hope had from the start been regarded as a second-best option. As already noted, Andrew Banks had sought to run from council-owned Burwick from whence the passage distance and time to Gills would have been much less. This would have enabled the frequency and, therefore, the capacity of the route to be increased, so further

Pentalina arriving at Gills Bay. *Photo R N Pedersen Collection*

The Swilkie. *Photo R N Pedersen Collection*

Andrew Banks (right) recounts his story to the author (left). *Photo R N Pedersen Collection*

The first long serving *St Ola* (1892–1951). *Photo circa 1950 courtesy of the late William Macdonald*

Blockships in Holm Sound and the start of the barrier's construction.
Photo RAF Reconnaissance 1943

Churchill Barrier No. 3 today. *Photo R N Pedersen Collection*

The second *St Ola* (1951–1975) discharging a car by derrick at Stromness in August 1962. *Photo Andy Wylie courtesy of Alan Hale*

The third *St Ola* as new in 1975, the first RO-RO ferry on the Pentland Firth.
Photo courtesy of Orkney Image Library

Above. Messrs Thomas & Bews' *Pentland Venture* at John O' Groats.
Photo R N Pedersen Collection

Right. Varagen on the day she was named by Lisa Tullock in 1989.
Courtesy of Edwin Rendall

Pentalina B at St Maragret's Hope. Photo R N Pedersen Collection

Placing the 'H' beam between the Gills Bay dolphins. *Photo courtesy of Andrew Banks*

Dredging at Gills Bay. *Photo courtesy of Andrew Banks*

The floating dock extension to Gills Bay pier with Stroma in the background.
Photo R N Pedersen Collection

NorthLink *Hamnavoe* arriving at Scrabster. *Photo R N Pedersen Collection*

Claymore at Gills Bay in February 2009. The floating dock extension, with digger on top, is on the right. *Photo R N Pedersen Collection*

Resplendent *Pentalina* just after launching at Cebu. *Photo courtesy FBMA*

Pentalina's controls. Note the four throttles to the right of the stack.
Photo R N Pedersen Collection

Pentalina at her home port of St Margaret's Hope. *Photo R N Pedersen Collection*

enhancing its attractiveness. Now that operational success had been demonstrated, Pentland Ferries again applied to Orkney Islands Council for a grant towards upgrading Burwick to allow a vehicle ferry to operate from it. This was refused in September on the grounds that the Scottish Executive had just approved vast sums of money for the upgrading of terminals for North-Link, the winner of the new Orkney and Shetland ferry tender. Andrew then offered to upgrade Burwick at his own expense but yet again the offer was rejected.

As the passenger certificate was for summer only, the service reverted to freight and 12 passengers at the end of October.

Not unnaturally with a new service, there were some teething problems. Exceptionally low tides at St Margaret's Hope delayed sailing times on occasion because *Pentalina B* loaded over the stern at St Margaret's Hope and although the pier had been dredged two years before, it had silted up somewhat since. It was hoped that the problem would rectify itself through time, as the ship's propellers stirred up the silt. A more serious issue was that despite the construction of the pier extension at Gills Bay for the vessel to lie against, Gills was still proving exposed to westerly winds and swells. This rendered the crossing prone to cancellation in bad winter weather. Rather than run an unreliable service, Andrew decided to withdraw sailings for winter from late November, pending a solution to the exposure problem at Gills Bay. The solution called for ingenuity. This was not lacking.

THE SECOND SEASON

The 2002 season, operating to the same schedule and prices as for the previous season, got off to a good start from 29 March, and, as the service had now become better known, it was running at full capacity by summer. Freight traffic also started to grow as the convenience of the schedule, low price and general reliability came to be understood within the haulage community. It became clear that, although Pentland Ferries' marketing budget was modest compared with that of P&O Ferries, a large section of the Orkney travelling public, increasing numbers of visitors from the south and hauliers were voting with their feet and wheels to travel on the short sea crossing. New business was being generated, but Pentland Ferries was also eating into P&O Ferries' carryings, which declined significantly from 47,000 cars per annum in 2000 to 37,500 in 2002. That summer season Pentland Ferries cleared around £1.5 million in revenue – a very satisfactory result.

The problem of silting at St Margaret's Hope had not gone away. The wash from the ship's screws did not resolve matters as had been hoped but in fact made things worse when, in March, a 20-foot section of the stone pier wall collapsed. Piling was brought over from Caithness and a quick repair was made. To resolve the silting issue Andrew set about dredging the harbour with his own Ackerman digger on a spud-leg barge. The method was simple. The barge with digger was towed to Andrew's small tug *Fara Lass* to a point adjacent to the pier after *Pentalina B* had departed. The digger dredged the silt from the ferry berth. Before *Pentalina B* returned, the barge was towed to a point adjacent to the approach road and the spoil deposited to create an expanded marshalling area.

Earlier chapters mention the Orcargo service between Kirkwall and Invergordon, provided by *Contender*. After that freight operation ceased, Andrew made it known that he hoped to re-open the Orkney–Invergordon route. To this end he sought a second ship and in August announced that he had bought the former CalMac ferry *Claymore*, then laid up at Birkenhead. *Claymore* had been built in 1978 by Robb Caledon of Leith for the Oban–Barra and Lochboisdale (South Uist) routes, serving also Coll and Tiree. Similar in size to *Pentalina B*, she did not have that ship's 'roll-through' capability but loaded vehicles over the stern only. All passenger accommodation was forward. The price was reasonable at £350,000, but as she was by then out of MCA Class (i.e. her passenger certification had expired) there would be a considerable cost in bringing her up to Class 8A, required to run with freight and 12 passengers to Invergordon. Andrew had the idea that, as Burwick was not for the present available to him, he could perhaps operate six return crossings per day on the Hope–Gills route with the two vessels. *Claymore* sailed north to St Margaret's Hope in October, suffering bad weather and engine problems en route. In November she commenced a daily Hope–Invergordon operation but this was not a success and the service stopped after three weeks. For the rest of the winter *Claymore* was laid up. For the winter of 2002–03 *Pentalina B* also operated on a reduced schedule as a 12-passenger freighter, as it would have cost too much to upgrade this far from youthful vessel to the year-round Class IIA passenger certificate standard. Financially, the success of the summer was undone by heavy losses on the winter operation.

WEATHER AND OTHER CONTINGENCIES

Winter sailings continued into 2003, with *Pentalina B* providing two return sailings daily from the Hope at 08:00 and 14:00. On 15 January a hurricane caused the cancellation of all sailings. She was back on station next day. Further bad weather at the end of January with a resultant heavy swell at Gills Bay caused *Pentalina B* to be diverted to Scrabster and Invergordon to carry essential Orkney supplies. This was all the more urgent as the trunk A9 road into Caithness was blocked by snow drifts and Caithness itself was cut off. Furthermore the stand-in Stromness–Scrabster vessel *Hebridean Isles* lay stormbound at Stromness for three days. During February and March, Scrabster runs were a regular feature.

Claymore as yet had not been completely upgraded to meet the new SOLAS (The International Convention for Safety of Life at Sea) regulations but she took over the route as a

12-passenger freighter in March to allow *Pentalina B* to go to Aberdeen for her annual overhaul. Unfortunately, four days later *Claymore*'s bow thruster failed as she approached the Hope on her evening run and she ran aground on her approach to the pier. With the aid of the Longhope lifeboat and Andrew's workboat *Fara Lass*, the 12 passengers were landed and *Claymore* was berthed safely. *Claymore* was withdrawn immediately for MCA inspection but back on service after one day's interruption to the service. The normal pattern of three return sailings recommenced on 1 April and on 4 April normality resumed once *Pentalina B* returned from Aberdeen with her 250 passenger Class VI certificate again in operation.

THE SAGA OF THE FLOATING DOCK

Following up Norman Moncrieff's earlier tip-off that snowy April in 2001 when *Pentalina B* had been in Lerwick for overhaul, Andrew contacted Malakoff and Moore to check whether or not the floating dock at Holmsgarth was in fact for sale. It was. A deal was struck, scrap value price agreed and Pentland Ferries became the proud owner of an enormous structure with the idea that it would be sunk at the seaward end of the pier extension at Gills Bay to form a breakwater. At 114 metres long by 23 metres wide (twice the width of the existing pier at Gills Bay) and 9 metres high, Andrew reckoned it would do the job.

If readers may permit a short digression, the concept of sinking floating structures onto a prepared base to form a permanent quay is not new and was patented in 1844 by Caithness man James Bremner, then a local Lloyd's agent. The same Mr Bremner suggested the construction of a beacon as a navigation aid at the south-west tail of Stroma, and the Commissioners of the Northern Lighthouse Board put one (unlighted) in place in 1857. Since the introduction of Pentland Ferries, the Northern Lighthouse Board decided to place a light on this structure for the first time – after 150 years.

In any event, in December, Andrew's floating dock was towed from Lerwick by the Invergordon-based tug *Kincraig* to St Margaret's Hope, where cranes were removed, the dry dock gutted, and oil and other contaminants removed. The huge unlovely structure, which for a period was to dominate the Hope, was then strengthened and shuttered with concrete at what would become the outer end of the breakwater, and a notch cut out of the inner end to enable the dock to marry with the existing pier. In the meantime the seabed location at Gills Bay for which the floating dock was destined was levelled by Holyhead Towage using two spud-leg barges. Site preparation was all important.

By late spring the floating dock was ready to be moved to its intended new location at Gills Bay. Again, a load line towing exemption certificate was required. The local SEPA (Scottish Environmental Protection Agency) surveyor gave environmental clearance. The MCA surveyor came to Orkney from Lerwick and he too expressed satisfaction, but, as an aside, he indicated that 'Aberdeen' wanted to be notified if Andrew tried to move the dock. And the dock could not be moved until Orkney Harbour Authority was provided with a copy of the exemption certificate. The implication of this was that once the dock was under tow, there would be a chain reaction: harbour authority–MCA Lerwick–MCA Aberdeen–Scottish Executive, followed by an order to prevent the dock being put in place at Gills Bay. A tricky situation!

As soon as the MCA certificate was received, it was faxed 'almost' immediately (but just after office hours) to Orkney Harbours. Meantime the tug *Kincraig* had been called in from Invergordon and as the tow was prepared, half the population of St Margaret's Hope assembled at the pier to watch the departure of the colossal floating structure, which took place at around midnight with *Kincraig* in the lead and Andrew's own tug *Fara Lass* in attendance. So far so good. But then things started to unravel – literally. The assemblage met a bank of thick fog off Stroma. Then the tow rope parted. A 3-mile chase ensued before an emergency line could be attached and the dry-dock brought under tow again by 6 a.m., with the additional assistance of an Orkney Towage Company tug. The fog was still thick, so that placing the dock into its planned position was out of the question. There was no alternative but to wait in the bay.

As the fog started to clear *Pentalina B* was spotted on the radar making her first morning run to Gills Bay. After she made her turnaround and was clear again by 10 a.m., the tugs were positioned to get the dock into its allotted place. *Kincraig* was pushing on the side of the dock with the Orkney tug on the back line. *Fara Lass* stood by to run lines ashore. The first attempt failed to get a true alignment; the same with the second. Then the third attempt got wires ashore. Diggers pulled on the wires. The dock fitted perfectly to the existing pier extension. The Orkney tug departed, and by line of sight *Kincraig* alone eased the dock into its exact alignment. At this the barge master Norman Moncrieff started the dock engines and commenced the flooding and sinking of the dock onto its prepared and levelled place on the sea bed. Success!

Congratulations were short-lived. Two fisheries officers arrived on site: 'You can't sink that thing there! We've been instructed by the Scottish Executive to stop the operation.' Andrew Banks, politely, slowly and softly explained: 'I'm afraid you're too late,' as bubbles issued from the nether regions of the dock and it slowly settled into its final resting place. The fisheries officers stomped off. Then there followed the menacing phone calls, threatening to send in a salvage company to remove the 115-metre colossus and to bill the cost to Andrew Banks. Civil servants in the Scottish Executive called an emergency meeting to discuss action.

This action brought the Northern Lighthouse Board into the picture. They are the body responsible for sanctioning aids to navigation in Scotland and the Isle of Man. The issue fell on the desk of the Northern Lights' Navigation and Business Manager, Kieran Nash, an ex-Royal Navy man. Fortunately, and perhaps atypically for a bureaucrat, Kieran is a man who instinctively sees the bigger picture. Unbeknown to Andrew at that time, Kieran was intrigued by Pentland Ferries' initiative from the business development point of view, and indeed saw the re-use of the floating dock as recycling at its best. All on a grand scale, and all the more commendable as the project was undertaken by private enterprise without requiring any public sector incentivisation. Kieran Nash was called to an urgent meeting in the Scottish Executive HQ at Victoria Quay: the Edinburgh civil servants were clearly of a very different opinion. Their prime concern seemed to be to class the dock as a danger to shipping that would, therefore, have to be removed. Reportedly, after preliminaries, the meeting went something like this:

'What can we do?' asked the troubled civil servant.

'Well as far as we are concerned the Gills Bay harbour facility is adequate and we are happy,' replied Northern Lights.

'So what can we do?' repeated the even more agitated civil servant.

The Executive lawyer intervened – 'I'm afraid we can't do anything.'

'So we've no power at all in this matter?'

'No.'

A couple of days later a man from the Commissioners of the Northern Lights arrived at Gills Bay. As it happened, the Gills harbour master was himself an ex-Northern Lights man. The two discussed the pros and cons of the situation, saw eye to eye and it was agreed that, so long as two green lights were placed at the seaward end of the dock, it presented no danger to shipping and was in fact a valuable aid to improving shelter on this otherwise exposed part of the Caithness coast. And so it proved: from that time, berthing at Gills Bay was a far easier matter. No doubt the bureaucrats were furious!

9

NORTHLINK

While Andrew Banks was applying every ounce of his energy, enterprise and ingenuity to set up, launch and operate Pentland Ferries without any help at all from the public purse, a sequence of events was unfolding at the western end of the Pentland Firth in which vast and ever vaster sums of public money were to be poured into propping up an ill-conceived rival ferry service.

THE TENDER

The government's contract with P&O Scottish Ferries was due to end in April 2002. One of the key issues to be taken account of in the new tender was the requirement to conform to new SOLAS regulations under the Stockholm Agreement. The SOLAS Convention originated in 1914 in response to the *Titanic* disaster, and it concerns the safety of merchant shipping. The new Stockholm Agreement specified stricter minimum standards for the construction, equipment and operation of merchant ships, and it had become clear that the older P&O vessels would not comply. The first steps in opening up what came to be known as the Northern Isles tender process commenced in late summer 1998, when the Scottish Office advertised for expressions of interest by potential operators. By March 1999 eight companies had expressed an interest in the contract and in the end invitations were sent out to six bidders. These were: Caledonian MacBrayne and associates; P&O Scottish Ferries; Red Funnel; Sea Containers; SERCO Denholm; and Stagecoach Holdings.

Meanwhile, the Scottish Office issued a consultation document to seek views on the type of service that was desired. Orkney Islands Council (OIC) Transport Committee made it clear that they wished Orkney to be considered separately from Shetland. While the tendering process was in train, the Scotland Act to re-establish the Scottish Parliament was passed in November 1998. The first elections were held in May 1999 and the new Scottish Executive assumed its full powers in July 1999, at the same time taking over most of the functions of the former Scottish Office.

Further representations were made later in the year but little was heard until December 1999, when Sarah Boyak MSP, the Scottish Executive Transport Minister, announced that four companies had been invited to tender. Red Funnel and Stagecoach Holdings had been dropped. Two of the conditions that had been made, after consultation, was that Scrabster–Stromness were to be the terminal ports for the Pentland Firth crossing and that this crossing should be by a vessel capable of making the passage in 90 minutes. These were to be very costly stipulations.

THE NEW KID ON THE BLOCK

The tendering process dragged on until 1 October 2000, when Sarah Boyak announced that the preferred bidder to operate the Northern Isles routes was 'NorthLink Orkney and Shetland Ferries' – a partnership between Caledonian MacBrayne and the Royal Bank of Scotland. Because of the delayed decision, the start date was set back to 1 October 2002, with a consequent end date of 30 September 2007. Even this extended timescale was short in the extreme because the new deal required the building of three brand new ships, each with a capacity for 600 passengers: one 18-knot, 110-metre, 8,600-ton vessel for the Pentland Firth and two 24-knot, 125-metre, 12,000-ton vessels for the Aberdeen–Orkney and Shetland routes. Fares were to be lower than P&O's, as was the agreed annual subsidy of £10,773,000 in the first year, reducing to £7,828,000 in the fifth. It seemed too good to be true – and it was, as time would tell.

In January 2001 contracts were agreed with the yard of Aker Finnyards in Rauma, Finland, for construction of the new ships at a cost of around £30 million each. A competition was held to decide the names of the new ships. Names of an appropriately Norse flavour were selected. The Pentland Firth ship was to be called *Hamnavoe*, the traditional name for Stromness. The two Aberdeen-based ships were to be called *Hjaltland* and *Hrossay*, Old Norse appellations for Shetland and Orkney respectively. Additionally, the name *Hascosay* was allocated to a freight and livestock vessel that the company proposed to purchase. Meanwhile £40 million plus of major terminal works were underway to accommodate the new ships, of which £13.8 million was attributable to terminal upgrading at Scrabster with a further £2.5 million for Stromness.

Details of proposed arrangements for the new services were announced bit by bit in the course of the year. Livestock was to be conveyed in 'cassettes' – specially designed double-decker wheeled containers. Freight rates, which were not supposed to be covered by the state subsidy, were, rightly, to be on a transparent per-metre basis in place of the variable secret deals offered by P&O, whereby preferred customers got heavily discounted prices whilst others paid 'through the nose'.

PROBLEMS

By autumn, Gareth Crichton, the company's new commercial director, gave the first hint that one of the Pentland Firth terminals would probably not be ready for the October 2002 deadline. In February 2002 storm damage to the piling at Scrabster set back reconstruction work to the extent that it became clear the terminal would definitely not be ready in time for the start of the new service. A stopgap arrangement was made to charter Caledonian MacBrayne's smaller and slower ferry *Hebridean Isles* to undertake sailings between Stromness and Scrabster until the terminal facility required for the much larger *Hamnavoe* was completed.

In September the two larger ferries *Hjaltland* and *Hrossay* arrived at Lerwick and Kirkwall respectively, where they were formally named and opened up with understandable pomp and ceremony for public inspection. The general reaction to the high standard of accommodation was favourable. *Hebridean Isles* arrived at Stromness on 30 September straight off overhaul in Aberdeen. On the following day, the new service commenced to a new three round trips per day schedule but, on account of her slower speed, with a two-hour passage time rather than the 90 minutes originally planned.

The experience of the first months of operation was mixed. Problems of sustained severe weather, a call centre incapable of handling the volume of bookings, competition on the Shetland route from a new rival, Norse Island Ferries, and vulnerability of Aberdeen Harbour to closure in bad weather adversely affected the Aberdeen–Orkney–Shetland services, but that is a story for another book. Bad weather also affected the *Hebridean Isles* on the Pentland Firth and many sailings were cancelled. It will be recalled, of course, that Andrew Banks's Pentland Ferries services had by this time been operating for a year and a half and had picked up much of the lucrative year-round haulage traffic. *Pentalina B* also suffered her share of weather cancellations, however, not least because Gills Bay had at that time not been extended and remained exposed to swell. On the Pentland Firth there was in that particularly windy winter of 2002/03 a degree of substitution of traffic from one carrier to the other depending on which was able to sail.

Some two and a half weeks into the *Heb Isles*' interregnum the £28 million *Hamnavoe* arrived at Stromness for naming and public inspection. As regards the quality and spaciousness of her passenger accommodation, she was and is undoubtedly much superior to any previous Pentland Firth ferry. This includes:

both à la carte and self-service restaurants, bar, shop and 16 staterooms (cabins) to enable passengers on early sailings to sleep on board overnight. At 8,600 tonnes, 112 metres' length and 18.6 metres' beam, she has a capacity of up to 600 passengers, 95 cars or 25 trailers. Her top speed of 20 knots is more than enough to meet the planned 90-minute schedule. The downside of all this largesse is that the large passenger capability necessitates a large crew of 28; the power to achieve 20 knots translates inevitably into an immense thirst for fuel (which even at 17 knots amounts to 1,835 litres per hour, so her daily consumption was equivalent to the *weekly* consumption of *Claymore*). Furthermore, the very high capital cost demands an unusually high annual fee to the Royal Bank of Scotland to cover capital repayment, interest and profit – an overall annual cost many times that of the Pentland Ferries operation.

In short, the Scottish Executive had agreed to a very expensive 13-year lease deal for the three NorthLink ships in a PFI (Private Finance Initiative) arrangement. As will be revealed, subsequent research by Napier University's Professor Alf Baird revealed that the vessels had been purchased at very high prices compared with the cost of similar and indeed much larger vessels bought by other operators around the same time. It seems that the conflicting irony of a major shareholder in NorthLink being the actual bank that was leasing the vessels to the state had been lost on the civil servants who had swallowed the deal. As the government was footing the bill, the bank naturally had little incentive to negotiate a lower price for the ships.

Sadly, *Hamnavoe* had to sail the following day to Leith for an extended lay-up because of the problems experienced by the Scrabster Harbour Trust in constructing their new pier to accommodate her. By February 2003 Bill Davidson, NorthLink's chief executive (and the former KPMG consultant who had engineered the ship lease deal between the bank and the Scottish Executive) was understandably frustrated. Work at Scrabster, which had been due for completion by August 2002, was still nowhere near ready. Following a crunch meeting with representatives of Scrabster Harbour Trust, the Scottish Executive and the contractors, it was agreed as a temporary measure to adapt the old (*St Ola*) pier at Scrabster to allow *Hamnavoe* to take up the station for which she had been built, albeit in favourable weather conditions only. The temporary works were undertaken and, by the middle of March, Bill Davidson was able to announce: 'Use of the old pier is a short-term solution and will be in operation only until the new pier is ready. A revised timetable for the *Hamnavoe* service will be introduced from April 21 and bookings for that date and beyond will take account of the new and improved arrangements.'

HAMNAVOE ENTERS SERVICE

And so it transpired. *Hamnavoe* was at last awakened from her long and expensive winter slumber in Leith from whence she departed on 7 April to arrive in Stromness late on 9 April, having called en route at Aberdeen, Lerwick and the new Hatston terminal at Kirkwall. She started scheduled operation between Stromness and Scrabster on 21 April allowing *Heb Isles* to return to her West Highland duties. *Hamnovoe*'s schedule gave three daily round trips on weekdays and two each on Saturdays and Sundays, with departures from Stromness at 04:15 (weekdays only), 09:00 and 17:00. With minor variation, this general pattern was maintained. Adult passenger return fares were £27.00 (low season), £30:00 (mid season), £33.00 (high season). Car return rates (with driver) were £98.00, £102.00 and £112.00 respectively, with reduced rates for additional car passengers.

In 2003 the price of oil was nothing like as high as it was to become in its 2008 peak but regardless of price, to put *Hamnavoe*'s thirst for fuel and concomitant carbon and other noxious emissions into perspective, her consumption of over 1,800 litres per hour is equal to no fewer than 2,700 litres for each single trip between Stromness and Scrabster. A typical annual traffic figure for the route of 42,000 cars per year is equivalent to an average of 20 cars per trip. That is 120 litres per car per trip of 25 miles, or around one gallon per car per mile! Bearing in mind that the average car does some 30 to 50 miles to the gallon, it is on average some *40* times more fuel efficient to drive a car 25 miles than to put it on *Hamnavoe*! If ever there was an argument for seeking the shortest ferry crossing, the relative fuel burn comparison is surely it.

The new terminal building at Scrabster was opened by Prince Charles, Duke of Rothesay in August and finally in September *Hamnavoe* was able to use the new pier, the final cost of which was £20 million (50 per cent over budget). Pentland Ferries was in essence competing against a public investment of over £50 million in terms of NorthLink's Pentland Firth ship and terminals.

LOSSES

By this stage it had become clear to the NorthLink management that the budget on which their tender had been based had been wholly unrealistic and, notwithstanding payment of the agreed subsidy, the whole operation was losing money and would be unable in all likelihood to survive the agreed tender conditions. By any normal commercial standard, the company was in Queer Street, if that old-fashioned expression may be permitted. It was then revealed in the September accounts that NorthLink had received an additional £1 million mainly to contribute to the cost of chartering *Hebridean Isles*. The reasons stated for the firm's woes were: the delayed availability of Scrabster (understandable); that they were given inaccurate figures by the Executive on the amount of freight being carried in and out of the isles (they should surely have done their own due diligence); competition from Norse Island Ferries to and from Aberdeen (less understandable, bearing in mind that that operation ceased in June 2003); and competition on the Pentland Firth from Pentland Ferries.

It was claimed that Pentland Ferries has reduced Stromness–Scrabster carryings by 30 per cent as compared with budget. It seemed to have been forgotten that Andrew Banks had purchased *Pentalina B* and announced his intention to operate on the Pentland Firth as early as 1997. This was fully a year before the Scottish Office advertised for expressions of interest by potential operators for the Northern Isles contract and even longer before views were sought on the type of service that was desired. One explanation that can be offered for NorthLink's misjudgement is that either the powers that be and/or North-Link didn't believe Andrew could 'pull it off' and commence operations, or if he did, he would be driven out by their financial muscle and political influence – a very bad and expensive mistake! In fact a senior employee of NorthLink did suggest as much to Andrew. Such an arrogant attitude does perhaps explain the intense hostility and obstruction met with by Pentland Ferries directly and obliquely by some representatives of national and local government at that time.

RE-TENDERING

In April 2004 Scottish Executive Transport Minister Nicol Steven MSP announced an early start to the re-tendering of the Northern Isles contract. In fact, because of NorthLink's difficulties an early termination (by nearly two years) of the extant contract was agreed. Then it was announced that NorthLink had been granted no less than an additional £13.4 million to tide them over until the end of the now truncated contract. A May deadline was set for expressions of interest in the new Northern Isles tender. Ten firms put their names forward, including NorthLink and Pentland Ferries. The process was to be a protracted one, during which large slugs of cash were doled out to keep NorthLink afloat.

In June 2005 the press reported a further £6.32 million subsidy 'top-up' to enable 'lifeline' ferry operator NorthLink to post a hefty profit in the previous year, and that, incredibly, surplus cash was not to be refunded to the taxpayer. If NorthLink failed to win a new contract to run services to Orkney and Shetland, the company would be wound up and any retained profits split between so-called joint venture shareholders Royal Bank of Scotland and Caledonian MacBrayne. It further reported that NorthLink had also received an additional £15 million of exceptional operating income over and above the agreed subsidy.

Then in July 2005 Scottish Transport Minister Tavish Scott MSP announced a short leet of three shipping companies who were to be invited to bid for the Northern Isles ferry services. These were V Ships UK Ltd, Irish Continental Ferries plc and Caledonian MacBrayne Ltd, the latter being wholly owned by the Scottish Executive and a 50 per cent shareholder in North-Link. That stakeholder, Royal Bank of Scotland, was withdrawing, leaving CalMac as the tendering company. The Royal Bank would continue to own the three ships *Hjaltland*, *Hrossey* and *Hamnavoe* which the winning contractor would be required to operate. Bearing in mind that other bidders had been excluded on grounds of poor financial performance, North-Link's inclusion as a potential contractor astonished many, as in just under three years the Scottish Executive had forked out £63 million to the company because of its inability to meet the financial obligations of its contract. The SNP called to have the matter investigated by the auditor general. MSP Jamie McGrigor expressed serious concern over the amount of public money given to NorthLink. 'I just hope the Scottish Executive has learned important lessons from its shambolic handling of the NorthLink Ferries fiasco, where they threw good money after bad to cover up their mistakes.' He might have added that over and above the vast and rapidly growing operating subsidy, some £50 million of public capital funds had been spent on terminals to accommodate the new NorthLink ships.

That same month the Transport Minister also revealed that a new freight contract for Orkney and Shetland would soon be put out to tender, to be operational the following year. The subsidy was not to apply on the Pentland Firth crossing.

In November the news broke that NorthLink Ferries was indeed under investigation by the Office of Fair Trading. OFT officials had made an unannounced visit to the company's offices in Orkney earlier in the month on an evidence-gathering exercise. An OFT spokesman said the agency had 'reasonable grounds' to suspect that the company had breached the Competition Act. The visits were part of an OFT investigation into allegations of the existence of a cartel involving ferry freight services. As part of their investigations OFT representatives met with Andrew Banks and the Gills Bay Harbour Association. The OFT report issued in November found no fault in the action taken when financial difficulties emerged. However, they did criticise the tendering process leading up to the appointment of NorthLink in December 2000. The report revealed that during the previous three years the Scottish Executive Transport Group (SETG) paid the basic contractual subsidy of £33.6 million. The contract allowed other payments of £16.7 million, which were made, along with £2.5 million, to pay off instalment leases on some of the assets used by NorthLink. Additional funding of £18.2 million had been spent simply maintaining service delivery – a total that by then had reached £71 million pounds in government subsidy, more than twice the amount agreed in the initial five-year contract. For some reason Andrew Banks and Gills Bay Harbour Association were omitted from the list of persons and bodies consulted – seemingly these, one would have thought, important witnesses were regarded as 'non-persons'.

Tavish Scott MSP welcomed the report and added that some lessons had already been learned and were part of the ongoing re-tendering process. It would be interesting to know even at this late stage what those lessons were.

NORTH SHIPS 'UNFIT FOR PURPOSE'

In January 2006 a damning report commissioned by the Northern Maritime Corridor (NMC) Project Group (funded by the EU Interreg IIIB North Sea Region Programme) emerged. The report drew attention to the excessive levels of government subsidy NorthLink was soaking up to keep the service going, at by then £78 million. Leading academic Dr (now Professor) Alfred Baird, of Napier University, who had drafted the report, explained that compared with most modern RoPax (high capacity RO-RO vehicle and passenger) ferries of over 120 metres in length, *Hjaltland/Hrossey* appeared to be two of the most inefficient and environmentally damaging ships built in recent years. This was because of their single freight deck and extremely high installed power, and hence very high fuel consumption and crewing relative to payload. The study advised that *Hjaltland* and *Hrossey* should be traded in for more efficient vessels.

Dr Baird calculated that using two standard 'Visentini-type' ferries, similar to the *Lagan Viking* operating between Birkenhead and Belfast, would save £10 million a year while virtually doubling freight/car capacity and giving space for more cabins, plus giving a more comfortable and reliable passage on the longer routes to and from Orkney and Shetland. They would also avoid the need to charter seasonal livestock vessels. He added: 'However, as Aberdeen harbour is incapable of accommodating larger RoPax ships of this length (i.e. 186m), in order to take advantage of these efficiencies it would be necessary to move the NE Scotland port call for Northern Isles services to nearby Peterhead, with the possibility of extending the service to Rosyth with its direct links to Europe.'

The report did not cover the Pentland Firth, but Andrew Banks pointed out that while he was making a profit with Pentland Ferries without a penny of public money, he could provide a *free* service across the Firth if given the proportion of

NorthLink's subsidy attributable to the Stromness–Scrabster service. This subsidy had been estimated at approaching £10 million per year. Thus if the Scottish Executive had acted on the NMC report and diverted traffic to the viable and efficient Pentland Ferries route by closing the Stromness–Scrabster route, it could have saved £20 million per year at a stroke, while giving an improved level of service. Tavish Scott retorted that no new boats were likely to be ordered to replace *Hjaltland* and *Hrossey* before the re-tendered six-year contract ran out. Andrew Banks's offer was ignored.

NEW CONTRACT – NEW NORTHLINK

On 6 July 2006 the Scottish Executive issued a press release stating: 'The six-year contract for lifeline ferry services to Orkney and Shetland has been awarded to NorthLink Ferries Ltd. The company takes over today, having been formed following the appointment of Caledonian MacBrayne, ferry provider on the west coast of Scotland, as preferred bidder.'

The new contract provided for: freight and livestock to be included for the first time; a mid-week freight call-in at Orkney; new livestock transporters from 2007; and an improved performance regime. It was awarded for a six-year period as a public service contract under the EC Maritime Cabotage Regulation and guidelines for state aid in the maritime sector.

David MacBrayne Ltd, in the ownership of Scottish Ministers (as is Caledonian MacBrayne), now owned NorthLink Ferries Ltd. The budgeted subsidy for the first year of operation was set at an incredible £31 million, subject to adjustments (upwards, inevitably) as necessary in the light of actual inflation and other factors provided for in the grant agreement – a blank cheque, to all intents and purposes! Thereafter, the subsidy was to be calculated according to the terms of the detailed grant agreement, which was issued in draft to the three companies invited to tender for the contract.

In welcoming the decision, NorthLink chief executive Bill Davidson, the former consultant who had engineered the un-folding financial disaster, said that the management team would stay the same and passengers were unlikely to see any great changes to the service. And so after the rigmarole of re-tendering, the company, essentially unchanged, that had so seriously misjudged its market, so extravagantly designed its ships, so avariciously consumed vast amounts of public funds, had been favoured by an inept Scottish Executive administra-tion with a further six years and an even vaster level of annual subsidy.

All the while, without any material support from national or local government, the Pentland Ferries operation tackled its own challenges and evolved to gain increasing support from the populace of Orkney and its visitors.

10

DEVELOPMENTS

From 1 November 2003, *Claymore* maintained the winter service, again as a freighter providing two daily return sailings. In January 2004 she gained her Class IIA certificate, enabling her henceforth to operate between St Margaret's Hope and Gills Bay all year round as a passenger ferry. She was permitted to carry 71 passengers in winter and 250 in summer. She commenced a revamped winter passenger schedule on 19 January on the basis of three daily round trips on the usual 08:00, 12:00 and 17:00 roster. *Pentalina B* in the meantime required substantial work on her engines and did not return to summer service until 3 June. From this point the rejuvenated *Pentalina B* ran to an enhanced summer schedule, offering four daily return crossings, with departures from St Margaret's Hope at 08:00, 12:00, 17:00 and 20:15.

This pattern of four return trips by *Pentalina B* in summer and three by *Claymore* in winter became more or less standard in ensuing years. While the improved service undoubtedly brought in additional custom, it necessitated the employment of additional crew to cope with the extended hours of operation in summer. Until this point fares remained as for the first season but for the first time, a high season (summer) fare structure was introduced, in line with most other year-round operators, of £12.50 per passenger and £27.50 per car – still the cheapest available. The inflation beating winter fare level of £10.00 and £25.00 has remained at the same level from the start of operations until the present day.

One advantage of the arrangement was that for much of the year, one or other vessel was available for charter. During 2006 and

2007 *Claymore* and *Pentalina B* were each chartered at different times by Albert Hall Farms of Yorkshire to carry livestock usually twice a week between Dover and Dunkirk and Boulogne.

ORCADIAN OF THE YEAR

If Pentland Ferries was not the toast of NorthLink, OIC or the Scottish Executive, there is no doubt that the company was a firm favourite with a large section of the Orkney population. In 2003 Kirkwall-based newspaper *Orkney Today* launched an annual trophy to recognise individuals who had made an out-standing contribution to the community. The winner for 2004 was none other than Andrew Banks, proprietor of Pentland Ferries. Early in 2005, the trophy was presented to Andrew in St Magnus Hall, the hall of Kirkwall's magnificent medieval St Magnus Cathedral. The trophy, which is sponsored by *Orkney Today*, Orkney Islands Council and Highland Park Distillery, is engraved with the following accolade:

Orkney Citizen of the Year Award 2004
For being an outstanding ambassador for Orkney
And a shining example to others

Besides the honour of holding the trophy for a year, with a small replica to keep for all time, Andrew was presented with a portrait of himself painted by celebrated Orkney artist Jenny Baines. The painting now has pride of place in the hall of *Ceol na Mara*, the Banks' family home in St Margaret's Hope.

Many who were aware of the hurdles Andrew had to over-come in establishing and maintaining Orkney's most convenient ferry link with the south could think of few if any who more deserved this recognition.

PLANS FOR A NEW SHIP

By 2005, traffic growth had pretty well reached the capacity of the vessels to carry it and patronage had begun to level out. One option would have been to run both the Pentland Ferries ships in summer, but this would have doubled the manning requirement and, therefore, the cost of operating the service for what may have been a marginal increase in revenue. In any case, neither ship was in her first flush of youth. The time had come to think about a new ship.

The quest for a new ship may be said to have started with a conversation with Professor Alf Baird, Orkney resident and oracle on up-to-date maritime policy. Professor Baird recommended that Andrew make contact with naval architect Stuart Ballantyne, managing director of Sea Transport Corporation – a celebrated Australian-based naval architectural consultancy specialising in modern vessel design. As his name suggests, Stuart Ballantyne M. Phil. Naval Arch. (Strathclyde) is a Scots Aussie. His credentials are impressive. They include seven years in the Merchant Navy as a deck officer, National Service with the Royal Australian Navy as a Sub-Lieutenant and Operations Superintendent with the Australian National Line prior to founding the Sea Transport Corporation in 1976. The group has developed innovative and highly cost effective designs for a wide range of commercial applications, from passenger- and vehicle-carrying catamarans to hydrographic research and other vessels which are now operational in 43 countries worldwide. The group has also developed a number of RO-RO ferry operations in Australia, and SeaSA, a subsidiary company directed by Stuart's wife Stephanie, was established to operate a successful RO-RO ferry service across South Australia's Spencer Gulf.

An exchange of emails and telephone calls ensued and in July 2005, Andrew met up with Mr Ballantyne at Harlingen in the northern Netherlands province of Friesland, where the pair inspected the new 64-metre passenger- and vehicle-carrying catamaran *Vlieland*. This vessel was designed by Sea Transport to ply to the West Frisian Islands in the Wadden Sea. She was built by FBMA Marine Inc. at Cebu in the Philippines to accommodate 1,200 passengers and 60 vehicles. She has a VIP

Lounge, tourist-class saloons, bar area and a large open sun deck. She was an impressive craft to behold, and in fact the vibrant colours of her interior decor won *Vlieland* the ShipPax Award for Outstanding Ferry Lounges of 2005. Fancy lounge or not, *Vlieland* clinched the idea in Andrew's mind of placing a catamaran on his Pentland Firth route.

Further discussions with Stuart Ballantyne ensued and in January 2006 Andrew set out for Australia to look at possible purchase of an Australian ferry. One call was to look over a ferry serving North Stradbroke Island, an hour from Brisbane. Another was catamaran *Seascape 1* at Adelaide, but neither was suitable for the Hope–Gills Bay run. On the way home he stopped off in the Philippines to visit the state-of-the-art yard at Cebu where a partially completed catamaran hull had been built on spec and was available for sale. FBMA Marine Inc. is an independent shipbuilding company that has, since its inception in 1997, established a name for delivering high- and medium-speed ferries, patrol vessels and specialist workboats to leading European, American, Australian and Asian shipping companies.

Negotiations commenced on the proposed purchase and adaptation of the half-completed vessel and Stuart Ballantyne looked at design and modification options. All this took time, and then a major stumbling block emerged, namely, that the twin hulls had been built with a single bottom, whereas the MCA insisted on a double bottom for operation in UK waters. The yard said they could modify the hulls accordingly but, after further discussion with Stuart Ballantyne and FBMA, it was decided, on Christmas Eve 2006, to go for a new purpose-built vessel to the required MCA specification.

The new-build option presented the chance for the first time to create a design specifically for Pentland Ferries' require-ments. In a nutshell, the company wanted higher capacity, higher speed, lower fuel consumption, lower operating costs and quicker turn-around times. The yard rose to the challenge and the specification was refined as follows:

Higher Capacity: at least nine truck or trailer spaces; 30 to 40 cars; 350 passengers in two separate lounges; sundeck; crew accommodation; capability for carrying hazardous goods vehicles, livestock, LPG tankers, etc on a section of open deck.

Higher Speed: crossing times from Gills Bay to St Margaret's Hope in less than 60 minutes and to Burwick in around 30 minutes; use of efficient turbo-charged high-speed diesels with low emissions and good sea-keeping in rough seas.

Lower Fuel Consumption: modern, efficient lightweight engines; optimising passenger space/power ratio; passenger space heating by heat recovery from main engines; optimising hull form design to balance sea-keeping with fuel economy and design optimised to limit vessel weight.

Lower Operating Costs: fewer crew required per payload; modern commercial equipment from European suppliers; lower maintenance costs and four engines with four propellers.

Quicker Turnaround Times: meet existing infrastructure and link-span configurations at Gills Bay, St Margaret's Hope and for other ports such as Burwick; no turning vehicles on deck; simplify vessel bunkering and restocking and ease of cleaning passenger areas.

The resultant design was a modern catamaran of a type wholly new to Scotland, with significantly greater capacity and speed than Pentland Ferries' existing vessels but at no greater operating costs. The comparison with NorthLink's *Hamnavoe* was stark. The speed and carrying capacity of the new vessel was to be only slightly less, but at £7 million, would cost a quarter that of *Hamnavoe* to build, would consume a third of the fuel and would employ a third of the crew.

A detailed comparison between the new vessel, *Claymore* and *Hamnavoe* is given at Appendix 1.

On 19 February 2007 Andrew Banks signed the contract for construction of the new ship with Doug Border, vice president of FBMA Marine Inc., and Craig Patrick, the yard's sales manager. The die was cast.

11

ADMINISTRATIVE NIGHTMARE

While the demanding business of developing the company was underway, it might have been reasonable to assume that things back at the St Margaret's Hope HQ would tick over as they had done for the previous few years. Unfortunately this was not to be the case.

Andrew's periodic absences from Orkney meant that he could no longer oversee the administration of the company's head office at St Margaret's Hope to ensure that the company was fulfilling its obligations in terms of maintaining the records and statistics required to satisfy the Maritime and Coastguard Agency (MCA). Andrew had recruited staff to cover this important aspect of the business. Despite this precaution, one of the most disturbing and sinister episodes in the company's short history was about to unfold. In fact events over the ensuing months caused such serious problems that the future of the whole enterprise was seriously endangered, lending credence to rumours then circulating that there was an active campaign to damage or destroy Pentland Ferries.

A key task for the next few months was to make sure that all the company documentation and records were up to date for the impending MCA audit. This is an important process, with which all shipping companies have to comply, particularly where carriage of passengers is involved. To award a passenger certificate the MCA must be satisfied that all the paperwork is in order. Andrew had been assured that the process was under control, but when the audit took place in October, the MCA were not happy with the state of the paperwork, so Pentland Ferries failed the audit.

Worse was to come, for despite further firm assurances that the paperwork would be up-to-date in time for the re-audit in December, it was not! The MCA found that the crew records were incomplete. The MCA auditor's words were: 'This is serious.'

The company had been given three months to sort out its documentation, and since the audit had failed a second time, the passenger certificate and the Document of Compliance could be withdrawn. Loss of the passenger certificate would mean the company's vessels would be restricted to operate as freighters only (limited to 12 passengers), but loss of the Document of Compliance would mean the company could not operate at all.

When Andrew explained that this would mean sacking all 50 employees and closing down the whole operation, the MCA man's response was: 'In the circumstances, I'll have to speak to Southampton.' The word came back that the passenger certificate was to be withdrawn as from 5 January, but for the present the Document of Compliance remained intact. One can imagine the level of festive gloom prevailing in the Banks household that Christmas. The two positive aspects of the situation were that the company was able to cater for the Christmas and New Year holiday rush and that at least January and February are normally quiet months as far as passenger traffic is concerned.

The MCA gave the company a further three months to get its affairs in order. Immediate remedial action was essential. Marine consultant Howard Goodrich of Myton Systems Ltd, based in Yorkshire, was taken on to sort out the paperwork and the office management. As he uncovered gaps and deficiencies, he realised there were serious problems with the new administrative arrangements. There were tensions in the office, where previously there had been a harmonious team spirit, and staff had started to leave. In any event, the documentation was brought up to standard for the next MCA visit in early April.

The reinstatement of the passenger certificate was a relief to all. Unfortunately, it came too late for the southbound Easter

Saturday sailings and 100 bookings had to be cancelled. This represented 300 passengers, necessitating 100 phone calls by Barbara and team at the Gills Bay office. She did a wonderful job. Such was the response from the public that almost all retained their return bookings and returned by Pentland Ferries. On the following day Andrew and Susan flew out to New York for a badly needed break.

Normal trading resumed, or so it was supposed. Yet troubled times were not over. One fresh setback followed another. Even on holiday in New York, a phone call from home revealed that an order for life rafts had been messed up. Was there no escape from this nightmare? On the Banks's return from America, and in anticipation of the eventual arrival of the new ship, work started on building new offices. This required demolition of a derelict silo. As work was ready to start on that, it transpired that the necessary permission had not been obtained for its demolition – something that should clearly have been attended to beforehand by the company's administrative personnel.

Then erupted a succession of complaints from all directions, including from Dover about *Pentalina B*, then on charter work on the Dover Strait, from Environmental Health in Orkney, and then most ominously from CHIRP indicating concerns about poor pay and conditions on Pentland Ferries vessels. CHIRP – Confidential Hazardous Incident Reporting Programme – is an independent confidential reporting programme for people employed or having an active interest in the aviation and maritime industries. CHIRP receives confidential reports and represents safety-related issues to the respective operational management and/or regulatory agency without revealing the identity of the reporter. Every one of these complaints was subsequently proven to have been malicious and unfounded.

The departure of one pivotal member of staff signalled a transformation and from that moment the company's management troubles ceased. In the ensuing tidy-up operation, the full horror of what had been going on emerged. This included letters discovered on the computer used by the recently departed staff member, falsely blaming Andrew for the lateness of documentation, and a handwritten note to be sent to the International Transport Workers' Federation (ITF) claiming low morale among the company's crews. It became increasingly clear that this one poisonous individual, whose actions had caused many a sleepless night, had intended serious harm to the business.

There was a silver lining to this vexed episode. A new management team was put in place. Harmony and efficiency were restored and the ensuing summer turned out to be a bumper season.

12

THE BURWICK ISSUE

In the summer of 2006, as the management of Pentland Ferries returned to something approaching normality, and with the prospect of a new, faster ship of greater capacity in sight, Andrew Banks felt it would be worth sounding out the Orkney Islands Council once more as to the availability of Burwick as an alternative to St Margaret's Hope. While the new ship would reduce the journey time from the Hope to Gills Bay to under an hour, the passage between Burwick and Gills Bay would be but half an hour, thereby enabling many more crossings to be made each day.

There is a well recognised effect in ferry economics that reducing passage time and increasing frequency has a significant effect on traffic generation. Experience worldwide shows that as a rule, easing traffic flow to and from an island population in this way brings substantial social and economic rewards to the island community. In other words, the more a ferry crossing resembles a road, the greater this beneficial effect.

THE THEORY OF ROAD TRAFFIC GENERATION

In simple terms, vehicular traffic on a road between two population centres is proportional to the population of the smaller settlement and inversely proportional to the square of the length of the road. Traffic flow will be further influenced by the quality of the road, e.g. single track = less traffic; dual carriageway = more traffic. In this way a traffic flow behaves like an electric current passing along a wire:

more Watts = more current (more traffic);
the longer the wire = more transmission loss (less traffic);
the thicker the wire = less transmission loss (more traffic).

Thus a road carrying traffic between two populations may be represented as in 'A' at Fig. 9 below.

Where one population is on an island and no ferry exists, the road may be represented as in 'B' below. In this instance a discontinuity occurs and no traffic can flow. Where a ferry bridges the discontinuity it can be represented as in 'C' in Fig. 9 below.

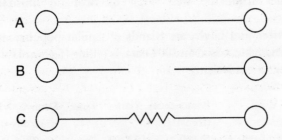

Fig. 9: The traffic generation diagram

The ferry symbol is shown as a 'resistor' in the 'circuit'. This is because traffic on a ferry is always less than on an equivalent free flowing road. The extent to which traffic is 'resisted' can be described as the 'impedance' factor.

THE THEORY OF FERRY IMPEDANCE

The impedance caused by a ferry crossing may be illustrated by comparing average daily traffic entering Caithness and Orkney respectively, viz:

	Vehicles	Passengers
Traffic entering Caithness	2,000	5,000
Traffic entering Orkney	275	825

Orkney and Caithness have similar populations, and if a road continued beyond Caithness to Orkney without interruption, one would expect Orkney traffic to be at least 50 per cent that of Caithness. In fact the ratio is 14 per cent for vehicles and 16.5 per cent for passengers, about one third that assumed for a direct road. This is the effect of impedance.

The degree of impedance can vary greatly, depending on the characteristics of the ferry service. The key characteristics of a ferry service are: passage time (combining distance and speed); frequency; hours of operation; and price. The following examples from the west coast of Scotland illustrate the effect.

Lismore and Gigha are islands of similar populations. The following table, based on 2004 data, is telling (fares are car single journey or equivalent):

Route	Passengers	Cars	Time (mins)	Return trips/day	Fare
Tayinloan–Gigha	54,000	12,500	15	7 to 10	£8.55
Oban–Lismore	13,000	2,000	50	3 or 4	£21.20
Pt Appin–Lismore (no cars)	56,000	0	10	14	

The combination of lengthy passage, low frequency and high charges result in severe impedance on the Oban–Lismore route as compared with the short, frequent, cheaper Tayinloan–Gigha service. The contrast between the two vehicle ferry routes is all the starker because the landfall for the Lismore vehicle ferry is Oban, a major regional centre, while that for Gigha is remote from even a local service centre. There are so many examples of the variability of this impedance effect in Scotland and worldwide that a near-formulaic relationship between time, frequency, cost and traffic growth can be taken as generally applicable.

Thus shortening the route between Gills Bay and the Orkney

landfall would simultaneously reduce passage time, increase frequency and ease traffic flow in and out of Orkney by providing much increased capacity at no extra cost.

THE COUNCIL'S RESPONSE

The Orkney Islands Council's Transportation and Infrastructure Committee met in September 2006 to consider a report from officials on the request by Pentland Ferries Ltd to lease Burwick Terminal. Significant points that concerned the council, as local Transport Authority, were that the information received from Pentland Ferries (e.g. on traffic figures) was not enough to enable the key issues to be addressed. Moreover, the 'lifeline' service between Stromness and Scrabster was franchised and subsidised by the Scottish Executive because there was supposedly no commercial service providing an adequate connection between Orkney and the Scottish mainland. If such a service did exist, the continuation of the current 'lifeline' service would be in question.

The council had to ensure that it achieved the best possible price in the disposal of any public asset. It claimed it could not therefore dispose of Burwick, by way of sale or lease, to one commercial interest, at a concessionary price. Also, leasing Burwick to one commercial ferry operator, which also controlled the nearest port in Caithness, could potentially give that company an eventual monopoly, unless they had agreements in place about frequencies, fares, etc pertaining to the lifeline route.

There was a possibility, too, that the council might itself wish to improve facilities at Burwick, to its own standards, making the improved facilities available to any user, not just Pentland Ferries.

The council decided it should remain the Harbour Authority for Burwick even if facilities were leased, and would still be responsible for the safety within the harbour area, and felt that 'extreme caution' would be needed in considering a lease to operate, as no formal risk assessment or simulation of port entry had been carried out recently by the Harbours Department.

As a result of these deliberations, the Committee decided to wait until all the relevant information had been received, and that the Director of Development Services should contact Pentland Ferries to get further details of their plans for future operations.

ANDREW'S REACTION

As may be imagined, Andrew was not overjoyed by the council's negative response. After consulting with Professor Baird, Pentland Ferries issued a press release dealing with the points raised by the council, highlighting two main issues: the Orkney Islands Council (OIC) was seeking to block Pentland Ferries' reasonable commercial request to use the available harbour at Burwick, and, in addition, OIC had openly stated that this action was related to the council's desire to protect the artificial competitiveness of the state-subsidised ferry service maintained by NorthLink Ferries between Scrabster and Stromness, so favouring one operator over another.

Andrew pointed out that OIC had originally developed Burwick Harbour so that it could be used for the short ferry crossing across the Pentland Firth. Burwick Harbour was open for business and was designed for ferries, and had plenty of spare capacity. He also made it clear that Pentland Ferries did not ask the council to 'dispose of an asset' but sought only to rent/lease space within the harbour, and that after all Burwick was a harbour facility advertised in the OIC Department of Harbours marketing brochure which, one would assume, was intended to attract potential users.

In referring to the possibility that the council might itself wish to improve facilities at Burwick, to its own plan and its own standards, making the improved facilities available to any user, an obvious question arose. Why not make these improvements now, when OIC had a willing port user and tenant, and an operator that was itself making substantial capital investments in a new vessel that would significantly improve access to and from Orkney? It was pointed out that Pentland Ferries intended to make capital investments approaching £10 million in ship and shoreside facilities to serve the people and economy of Orkney, yet the company did not ask for, nor expect, financial support from OIC or from other public agencies. The Pentland Ferries press release stated: 'Any other firm in any other industry contemplating such a multi-million-pound investment in Orkney, with significant economic impacts resulting, would be guaranteed substantial public sector support and encouragement. Conversely, all Pentland Ferries receives from OIC is discouragement, obstruction, and inertia.' In terms of the works required at Burwick, Pentland Ferries was satisfied that compared with the £37 million that was poured by the state into NorthLink's Orkney/Caithness terminals at Hatston, Stromness and Scrabster, any port investment at Burwick would be minuscule. The final section of Pentland Ferries' rebuttal of the council's response is below quoted in full:

Pentland Ferries' operation of a ferry terminal within Burwick Harbour would be covered by the company's own insurances, thereby limiting any OIC liability (another red herring!). Pentland Ferries' operations are already highly regulated and conform to all relevant safety standards, both onboard and ashore. The company would hardly enter into an agreement to rent a berth at Burwick if it was not certain that the harbour was fully capable of accommodating its vessels. Burwick was initially built by OIC to accommodate ferries and Pentland Ferries will only be using the harbour to accommodate its vessels. OIC's 'concerns' here are no more than exaggeration and scaremongering.

By refusing or delaying Pentland Ferries' reasonable request for access to Burwick Harbour, and by publicly stating its intention to do all it can to protect a competing ferry operator (subsidised/state-owned or otherwise), OIC is therefore intentionally (and most probably illegally) constraining the commercial functioning of Pentland Ferries and hence distorting the market. In doing so, OIC is effectively abusing its powers as both a port authority and as a local authority.

The reason why OIC is refusing/delaying Pentland Ferries' access to Burwick is clearly to placate vested interests, primarily the Scottish Executive (as ultimate owner of NorthLink Ferries) and OIC itself, who publicly maintains its support for what is a far longer, more exposed and hence more uncomfortable ferry service (i.e. Scrabster–Stromness), and which involves far higher operating costs, and of course in turn demands ever-increasing subsidy levels (i.e. taxpayers' money). The only thing that the NorthLink ferry service demonstrates is that Government should not be permitted to operate ferries; rather like the state's withdrawal from operating aircraft, trains, trucks and buses over the last 25 years, so there is now also an urgent need for the state to withdraw from the ferry business. The European Commission has in recent years urged Member States to withdraw entirely from operating state-owned ferry companies (though maintaining subsidies to private operators if need be), but in Scotland the role of the state in this respect has been increasing of late, and this goes against international trends.

A port authority that refuses any shipping company reasonable access to a harbour (particularly a harbour with spare capacity) on the grounds that this could adversely affect a competing service (subsidised or otherwise), is an act that would most likely be declared illegal by the courts. This is in part based on the well established Essential Facilities Doctrine as related to ferry harbours and . . .

On this basis, apart from doing a great disservice to the people and economy of Orkney, OIC's refusal to allow Pentland Ferries' reasonable request for early access to Burwick Harbour is misguided. Consequently, Pentland Ferries proposes that OIC as port authority should as a matter of priority make every effort possible to permit the company to operate its service from Burwick Harbour in the near future.

Fighting talk, but one can understand the frustration felt by Andrew at the sheer obfuscation on the part of the council in trying to prevent the development of a step change improvement in the level of access to the wider world available to its own population. However, change was in the air.

13

CHANGING TIMES

The new year of 2007 brought with it a growing sense of optimism. In February the contract for construction of Pentland Ferries' new catamaran ferry was signed and the world then knew, if it hadn't known before, that Andrew meant business. Then in May there were elections for the Scottish Parliament and the Scottish local authorities. For the first time, the business-friendly Scottish National Party (SNP) was able to form a minority administration nationally, ending some 50 years of Labour domination of the Scottish body politic. The new administration adopted the term 'Scottish Government' for general use in place of the former 'Scottish Executive'. In local government too there were sweeping changes and a sense that perhaps new ideas might be looked at.

ORKNEY EXPRESS

In September HITRANS (the Highlands and Islands Transport Partnership) and OIC jointly set out a proposal to provide a major upgrade of the Orkney bus network and to integrate it with other transport services. This proposal was part of the Bus Route Development Grant (BRDG) scheme that had been set up by the previous administration, and it sought a total of £1.7 million to upgrade the quality of vehicles, schedules, infrastructure, information, promotion, etc. But most significantly for this story, it proposed the introduction of a new express coach service between Orkney and Inverness via the St Margaret's Hope–Gills Bay ferry. This was the first time that the

Pentland Ferries service had been formally recognised in terms of practical action by OIC and HITRANS as an integral part of the public transport system. There was also a formal acceptance that the Stromness–Scrabster route was, at least in some respects, inferior to the Gills Bay crossing.

This was indeed a breakthrough. The proposal recognised that surface travel between Orkney and the Scottish mainland had been limited for travellers without a car. To travel from Kirkwall to Inverness by surface transport year round necessitated a bus journey to Stromness (no connection with the first ferry), NorthLink ferry to Scrabster, bus to Thurso and train to Inverness. At each interchange point passengers had to load and unload their luggage. With the proposed new service, passengers on a through ticket would load their luggage onto the high-quality coach at the start of their journey and would not have to pick it up again until they reached their destination, as the coach itself would travel on the ferry. The new route was to offer two return journeys between Kirkwall and Inverness every day, allowing day trips in each direction.

This proposal was approved by the various government funding bodies for introduction following the arrival of the new catamaran in summer 2008. In the event, the new vessel was delayed and the service did not go ahead as planned.

SCOTTISH GOVERNMENT ACTION

After years of complaints about how ferries in Scotland had been managed and subsidised, the new SNP government embarked upon three initiatives in an effort to get to the bottom of things.

Firstly, the Scottish Parliament's Transport, Infrastructure and Climate Change Committee was to hold an inquiry into ferry services in Scotland, investigating the usefulness of current ferry routes and the potential for new routes; the frequency and convenience of services; and the capacity of services and routes to meet the needs of ferry users. It was also to look into how well these routes integrated with other services, such as buses, and how much competition affected ferry services. Over and above these issues, the Committee wanted to hear views on any other subjects relating to ferry services in Scotland. Committee members embarked on a series of fact-finding visits. Then in February 2008, the Scottish Government Transport Minister, Stewart Stevenson MSP, announced that the Scottish Government was looking to overhaul the current ferry fares system and replace it with a fairer 'Road Equivalent Tariff' (RET) scheme which would bring cheaper travel for islanders, tourists and businesses across the country. I was particularly interested in this initiative as, back in 1974, when I was a young transport research officer with HIDB, I was the original architect of the RET concept. A pilot scheme would operate from October 2008 until the spring of 2011 on the Western Isles to mainland routes, resulting in up to 50 per cent off fares. There were complaints from Orkney and Shetland that they were being disadvantaged by exclusion from the trial, until it was pointed out that Orkney and Shetland already had fares in many cases lower than the RET as a result of the massive subsidy to NorthLink. Furthermore, the all-important frequency of service across the Pentland Firth was markedly superior to any ferry service to or from the Western Isles.

Two months later attention turned to Europe. Complaints had been made to Brussels in 2004–5 by 'unnamed third parties' that subsidies provided to NorthLink and Caledonian MacBrayne by the former Scottish Executive were illegal. It does not require much speculative effort to deduce that such complaints may have emanated from sources not far removed from Pentland Ferries, Gills Bay Harbour Association and Western Ferries on the Clyde, who had long been victims of subsidised competition from Caledonian MacBrayne/NorthLink. Matters were exacerbated by drawn-out wrangles, claims and counterclaims over the contentious method of tendering CalMac's

Clyde and West Highlands and Islands services. To tackle the issue head on, SNP Member of the European Parliament Alyn Smith took the dramatic step of urging the European Transport Commissioner and Vice-President, Jacques Barrot, to undertake a formal investigation of the 'state aid' given to Scotland's nationalised ferry operators.

Before considering the implications of these initiatives for Pentland Ferries, it is first necessary to look at the background to the development of ferry services in other parts of Scotland.

14

DEVELOPMENTS ELSEWHERE IN SCOTLAND

The extraordinarily unequal treatment by past Scottish administrations of Pentland Ferries and NorthLink has parallels beyond the Pentland Firth – namely the islands and peninsulas off the west coast of Scotland – the fiefdom of Caledonian MacBrayne. Some understanding of the development of ferry services in that area is necessary to appreciate why things are as they are in the north.

THE HISTORICAL BACKGROUND

The origins of commercial powered navigation in Europe date back to 1812. In that year, one Henry Bell, a Helensburgh hotelier, launched his pioneer steamboat *Comet* to ply the waters of the Clyde and in due course those of the West Highlands. From this modest beginning, Scotland, and the Clyde in particular, led the world in ship design and powered maritime development over the next hundred years. It was not long before a network of steamer services was developed from Glasgow and Greenock to the Clyde coast and the West Highlands.

In those early years the Firth of Clyde was a kind of proving ground for new ideas in the development of steam navigation. A fleet of competing fast paddle steamers vied for business between Glasgow and the various Clyde coast burghs and resorts. For much of the nineteenth century individual private operators were the norm, but by the end of the century the three railway companies that had railheads on the Firth created and operated their own fleets of fast, modern steamers in connection with their trains, thereby hastening the demise of the individual private owners. In 1923, the railways were grouped into four large Britain-wide concerns of which two, the LMS and LNER, took over the Clyde routes. In 1948, the railways and railway steamers were nationalised, bringing virtually the whole Clyde and Loch Lomond railway fleets and also the Kyle–Kyleakin (Skye) ferries under a single state ownership. In due course all these railway boats were managed under the auspices of the Caledonian Steam Packet Company (CSPCo) – originally a subsidiary of the Caledonian Railway but by that stage part of the state-owned Scottish Transport Group.

Developments in the West Highlands took a somewhat different turn. In 1851 the bulk of steamboat trade there was consolidated under the ownership of Messrs David and Alexander Hutcheson and in 1879 the business was carried forward by their partner, the legendary David MacBrayne, in his own name. With his flair for publicity, traffic expanded, particularly in catering for 'society' summer tourist trade on the 'Royal Route' by 'swift steamers' that supplemented the slower year-round passenger, cargo and mail services. The pattern of routes evolved over the next half-century as railhead connections to and from Oban, Kyle and Mallaig gradually supplanted 'all the way' sailings from Glasgow.

By the late 1920s, the MacBrayne fleet was elderly and criticised as unfit for modern conditions. Unable to finance replacement tonnage from earned revenue and the mail contract, the company was taken over jointly by the LMS Railway and Coast Lines and re-formed as David MacBrayne (1928) Ltd. The new concern was obliged to reorganise its services and build new ships. In 1948, simultaneously with the nationalisation of the railways, another West Highland operator, McCallum Orme Steamers, was absorbed by David MacBrayne. Further change came on the back of a 1952 white paper which provided a subsidy to the company of £360,000 per annum, subject to certain conditions, which included substitution of road services for many of the cargo ship calls.

In 1951 the British Transport Commission announced a £1,000,000 plan to modernise Clyde services. This resulted in the building of seven new motor ships of which three (introduced in 1953/54) were fitted with electric lifts or hoists to enable motor vehicles to be driven on and off at any state of the tide. This was an advance on former arrangements for carrying vehicles across the Firth, albeit still a somewhat slow and cumbersome procedure. A fourth and larger such vehicle ferry was added to the fleet in 1957. In 1960 Highlands and Islands Shipping Services Act made provision for subsidising shipping services operated by David Mac-Brayne under the terms of an 'undertaking' which was reviewed annually. That same year MacBraynes announced proposals for the introduction of three vehicle ferries to operate between Oban and Craignure (Mull); Mallaig and Armadale (Skye); and a triangular route serving Uig (Skye), Tarbert (Harris) and Lochmaddy (North Uist). The ferries were built for the government and leased to the company at commercial rates. Again this was an advance but, as hoist equipped side-loaders like the Clyde ferries, these vessels were by no means state of the art, bearing in mind that more efficient sea-going end loading RO-RO ferries had been in operation in North America since before the First World War.

NEW IDEAS

Until this time cargo on ships was charged according to a complex commodity scale based on tonnage or per item. In 1961 the Highland Panel recommended that charges to remote mainland centres should be used as a yardstick for determining sea service charges. This concept came to be known as the 'mainland comparison'. Pressure from the Panel in promoting this and other ideas resulted in the government of the day setting up the Highland Transport Board.

Meantime in 1963, a report to the Ministry of Transport, the Secretary of State for Scotland and the Minister of Aviation – *Transport Services in the Highlands and Islands* – noted that the introduction of vehicle ferries would, on the one hand, increase the need for government assistance to cover annual charges, but on the other hand, development in new traffic and rationalisation of services would in time reduce the need for grants. The report pointed out that the annual grant to MacBrayne was paid on social grounds, 'because without this help necessary transport services could not be maintained throughout this area at rates which traffic could bear'. The report noted the need for services and facilities to be progressively developed and that 'unless the Highlands and Islands are provided with adequate modern transport they will fall further behind the rest of the country'. The report noted that improvement would involve radical change.

The Highland Transport Board, under the chairmanship of Lord John Cameron, was appointed in December of the same year (1963) and in its 1967 report *Highland Transport Services*, made a number of radical recommendations affecting all modes of transport in the Highlands and Islands, including recommendations for Orkney as described earlier. In considering the 'mainland comparison' concept, the Board reiterated the Highland Panel's view and recommended that 'for the purpose of deciding the need for subsidy to shipping companies, the Secretary of State should adopt the criterion that the general level of charges to islands should not be materially in excess of charges to distant parts of the mainland'.

A further concept stressed by the Board was the Norwegian experience of vehicle ferry operations and in particular that of the Norwegian fylke (county) of Møre and Romsdal, whose chief roads surveyor, Mr K H Oppegård, had recently recommended the adoption of simple Norwegian-style roll-through vehicle ferries in Shetland. The essence of the Norwegian approach is selection of the shortest crossings with standardised vessels and terminals, resulting in low operating costs, high frequency and low fares. The technique was adopted in Shetland by a new private operator, Western Ferries, firstly to Islay and subsequently on the Clyde, but not elsewhere in Scotland.

The Highland Transport Board's report was submitted to the newly appointed Highlands and Islands Development Board (HIDB). The HIDB considered it and prepared a detailed paper which described how a meaningful 'mainland comparison' might be realised. The HIDB concluded that the simplest solution would be:

> to create conditions for transport to the islands which are truly comparable with those on the mainland. This means considering the appropriate ferry and shipping links as roads or bridges. The car ferry to an island and the piers are, in fact, parts of a flexible road over which cars and commercial vehicles can pass to and from islands.

The paper, which also recommended that a scale of lineal charges on vehicles on RO-RO ferries should replace commodity charging, was submitted to the Scottish Development Department in 1968, and after four years of correspondence and discussion, the government's decision was announced by the Secretary of State in a parliamentary statement in 1972. The statement maintained the principle that charges levied on sea services should be based on operating costs; it agreed to the introduction of RO-RO ferries and to linear charging for vehicles but it rejected the Norwegian concept that ferries should be regarded as part of the road system.

A year later, in 1973, the Caledonian Steam Packet Company Ltd was amalgamated with the greater part of David MacBrayne Ltd to form Caledonian MacBrayne (CalMac). The new company, then part of the nationalised Scottish Transport Group (STG), was made responsible for most of the regular shipping services and cruises on the Firth of Clyde and the West Highlands and Islands. It was expected that these services would be operated on a commercial basis, i.e. cover their costs from revenue. The new company was committed to conversion of most of its routes to RO-RO and in that year a new RO-RO Stornoway–Ullapool route was opened by the then new ferry *Iona* (later to become *Pentalina*

B), replacing the traditional Stornoway–Kyle–Mallaig mail service. This was the first modern 'roll-through' service to be
operated by the company. Although also part of the STG, a rump
of the old David MacBrayne Ltd remained to operate certain
unviable services with continuing subsidy under the 1960 Highlands and Islands Shipping Services Act.

By the 1970s the growth and then dominance of road transport did cause a fundamental reorientation of shipping services
with the gradual introduction of end-loading roll-on/roll-off
(RO-RO) vehicle ferries to supersede the old style of operation.
The effect of this was indeed to connect island road systems
with the mainland road system, albeit infrequently, and at
considerable cost to the user. The introduction of RO-RO
ferries made possible the introduction of a simple system of
lineal charging on vehicles to replace the old and complex
commodity-based cargo rates. It had been hoped that this
change would have the effect of reducing the cost of transporting at least full lorry-loads to the islands, but this was found in
practice not to have been the case.

Concern about the burden of freight charges to island
economies intensified and in 1974 the HIDB re-examined
the issue. Case study analysis revealed that in many cases island
business was indeed disadvantaged by sea freight charges. The
HIDB case was re-stated and refined in its 1974 paper *Roads to
the Isles – A Study of Sea Freight Charges in the Highlands and
Islands*. In this document, written by the author of this book, the
concept of 'Road Equivalent Tariff' or 'RET' was born.

A simple formula was created to translate this concept into a
lineal ferry charge. When compared with existing fares at that
time, it was noted that the general effect was that passenger fares
would remain broadly in line with those then obtaining but
vehicle rates would be generally at a lower level than those then
in force, particularly for commercial vehicles. In the event RET
excited much interest but was ultimately rejected by the government on grounds of expense.

DEBATE AND DEVELOPMENT

The HIDB's 1975 *Highlands and Islands Transport Review*, which I also drafted, set out a raft of transport policies for the area. This sought to reduce the economic disparity between the Highlands and Islands and the more affluent areas of the UK and the EEC. A further unpublished HIDB consultative paper of 1978 on ferries set out a more refined and detailed analysis of how the ferry system might be improved to the benefit of island economies in cost-effective ways. The concept of 'road equivalence' was expanded by setting out a programme based on Norwegian principles: adopt the shortest practical crossings; introduce economical Norwegian-style standardised vessels (designs were outlined); develop capacity through frequency rather than size of vessel; control costs (capital, crew, etc); allocate routes to operators by means of competitive tender; allocate subsidies by route rather than by operator; and require mandatory annual reporting of operating costs according to set standards.

Unfortunately, this programme was not instituted throughout Scotland, but Shetland and Western Ferries did follow it up, and traffic volumes soared while subsidy per passenger or per vehicle fell or ceased, benefiting these local economies.

Since then, various reports and individuals have suggested adoption of the above progressive and cost-effective methods but CalMac's operational approach has remained that of an old-style shipping company, rather than a modern ferry provider. They have continued to pursue a big ship, big crew policy, resulting in low frequencies, low volumes and high costs. It is interesting that in recent discussions with Stuart Ballantyne, designer of *Pentalina*, he revealed that he had, for some 20 years, paid annual visits to CalMac to try to persuade them to consider more cost-effective designs for their vessels, only to be met with blank incomprehension and ridicule.

15

WESTERN FERRIES

There was one quarter where more progressive ideas found favour. That quarter was Western Ferries. Its genesis was the creation of a new company, Eilean Sea Services, formed by Gavin Hamilton, Christopher Pollok and John Rose, who sought to prove that there was an alternative to the traditional method of shipping freight. They commissioned a new landing craft-type vessel, *Isle of Gigha*, in 1966 – just in time to take advantage of the seamen's strike of that year. She sailed mainly between Oban and several of the Inner Hebrides, clearly demonstrating the potential for a roll-on/roll-off ferry service. Tragedy struck, however, when she capsized that winter with the loss of two lives. *Isle of Gigha* was subsequently recovered and went on to have a successful career in West Highland waters for many years thereafter.

LEADERS OF THE RO-RO REVOLUTION

To develop the RO-RO concept further, a new company, Western Ferries, was registered in 1967 with a more substantial capital base. The company immediately ordered a new vessel and started construction of a simple purpose-built terminal at Kennacraig in West Loch Tarbert (Argyll). The new ship, *Sound of Islay*, launched in February 1968, was a functional stern-loading ferry of Norwegian design capable of carrying 25 cars or six commercial vehicles and up to 75 passengers – Scotland's first true RO-RO ferry. *Sound of Islay* launched a new service to Port Askaig in Islay in April 1968 in opposition to the traditional David MacBrayne lift-on/lift-off mail steamer *Locheil*. The new service was an immediate success. Two return crossings per day were offered and the famous island distilleries were quick to seize the advantage of bringing in their barley and exporting their distinctive 'water of life' by trailer rather than by the time-honoured but inefficient lift-on/lift-off alternative. Locals and tourists too were attracted by the simplicity and lower price of RO-RO. By summer, the need for a larger vessel was clear and an order was accordingly placed with the Norwegian yard Hatto Verkstad.

The new vessel, named *Sound of Jura*, commenced service in August 1969. She was of standard Norwegian design with a carrying capacity of up to 250 passengers and 36 cars or eight trailers, and with her greater speed of 14 knots, three round trips per day were offered. That same year *Isle of Gigha* was purchased by Western Ferries, renamed *Sound of Gigha* and placed on a new shuttle service between Port Askaig and Jura, thereby offering Jura a thrice-daily mainland connection compared with the thrice-weekly offering by David MacBrayne. Clearly Western Ferries was mopping up.

To be fair to the old David MacBrayne company, it had been in negotiation since 1966 with the then Argyll County Council to institute a new RO-RO ferry on a shorter route to Islay and Colonsay from a new deeper terminal at Redhouse near the mouth of West Loch Tarbert. Negotiations were protracted but a new purpose-built vessel was ordered in 1968. Then Argyll County Council backed out of its commitment to provide the new terminal. Without the new terminal the new ship could not be put on the Islay service because she was too deep of draught to use the existing shallow water pier at the head of West Loch Tarbert. The matter was resolved with the formation of the Scottish Transport Group (STG) in 1969, which brought David MacBrayne and the Caledonian Steam Packet Company under single ownership. This enabled CSPCo's hoist-loading car ferry *Arran* to be redeployed from the Gourock–Dunoon route to serve Islay in exchange for the new ferry *Iona*, which henceforth swapped places to take over between Gourock and Dunoon. This *Iona* is the self-same vessel that became Pentland Ferries' inaugural vessel, *Pentalina B*. *Arran* may have been an improvement on the Islay station, but she was no match for the smart, low-cost Western Ferries operation.

By the end of 1971 the then Secretary of State Gordon Campbell announced that because of losses sustained by the MacBrayne service he intended to withdraw subsidy for Islay and would leave Western Ferries as sole operators on the route. What happened next is a complex tale that deserves a book of its own. There are many parallels with the NorthLink–Pentland Ferries saga but suffice it to say that the newly formed Caledonian MacBrayne stayed on the Islay route and ordered a new fast ship *Pioneer* to 'take on' Western Ferries. The comparative statistical characteristics of the two vessels are set out in Appendix 1. In short, *Pioneer* required three and a half times the crew and about thrice the fuel for similar carrying capacity, or in the case of vehicles, less carrying capacity, than *Sound of Jura*. Only with a large guaranteed subsidy and predatory pricing was CalMac, with such an extravagant ship able to drive unsubsidised Western Ferries off the route in September 1976 – a blatant case of unfair subsidised competition.

Meantime Western Ferries found other fish to fry. For a time *Sound of Islay* was redeployed to pioneer a new route between Campbeltown, Kintyre and Red Bay, County Antrim in Northern Ireland, then she was employed on lucrative contracts in connection with the oil industry. When these contracts dried up and the Islay service stopped, *Sound of Islay* was sold to Canadian owners in 1982. Another venture by this innovative company was the introduction of *Highland Seabird*, Scotland's first fast (27 knot) catamaran passenger ferry. This Norwegian vessel of a type commonplace in Norway was tried on a number of passenger routes around the Clyde and West Highlands and for a time in the profitable business of transporting workers to

Kishorn oil platform fabrication yard. She also found intermittent employment in the Solent, Mersey and Irish Aran
Islands, with mixed results. She was eventually sold in 1985
to Emeraude Lines of St Malo. One venture above all was to
secure the future of Western Ferries, and that stemmed from
the purchase by the company of Hunter's Quay pier near
Dunoon in 1969.

THE CLYDE–ARGYLL ROUTE

In 1971, Western Ferries was in negotiation with Dunoon Town
Council to open up a RO-RO service from Dunoon in place of
the CSPCo's hoist-loading service to Gourock but, on the
casting vote of the provost, the CSPCo retained the privilege.
Then the decidedly odd decision was made to equip Dunoon
Pier with a link-span at right-angles to the face of the pier,
interfacing with *side* ramps on new vessels to be designed for the
route and so slowing the loading of vehicles, particularly large
commercials. The STG Annual Report of 1972 even went so far
as to say 'Dunoon Burgh Council are to be commended for their
vision in adopting this principle'.

This blunder was sufficient to encourage Western Ferries to
operate its own drive-through service from its own terminal at
Hunter's Quay on the shorter crossing to McInroy's Point, on
the outskirts of Gourock. In the spring of 1972 work started to
create *end*-loading capabilities at either terminal. That same
year, two second-hand double-ended Swedish ferries were
purchased. The first was *Olandssund IV* with a carrying capacity
for 25 cars and 200 passengers. In June 1973, after delivery from
Sweden, extensive overhaul and renaming as *Sound of Shuna*,
she started plying the route, giving an hourly service from 07:00
from Hunter's Quay to 23:30 from McInroy's Point. The one-
way fare was £1.00 for a car and 25p for a passenger. Caledonian
MacBrayne, the successors of CSPCo, immediately reduced
their fares on their parallel route. A month later the second,

smaller, Swedish ferry *Olandssund III*, capable of carrying 20 cars and 100 passengers, started to provide an enhanced half-hourly service at weekends. She had been renamed *Sound of Scarba*. In the six months to the end of the year Western Ferries had secured 34 per cent of cars moving between Inverclyde and the Cowal penninsula. The competing CalMac service was worked by *Glen Sannox* and *Maid of Cumbrae*, however, where the Western Ferries' vessels each had a crew of four, the *Glen Sannox* had a crew of no fewer than 27!

By summer 1974 traffic on Western Ferries' Clyde–Argyll ferry service had grown to such an extent that a half-hourly service was now required daily at morning and evening peaks and a midnight service was now provided from McInroy's Point. A third second-hand ex-Isle of Wight ferry, *Lymington*, was purchased for the service that year and she entered service as *Sound of Sanda* with a carrying capacity of 400 passengers and 26 cars. Other vessels were added to the fleet in ensuing years.

In 1974 too, the newly formed CalMac placed its new 38-car side-loading, so-called 'streakers' *Juno* and *Jupiter* on their longer but adjacent Dunoon–Gourock route on a half-hourly frequency. By the early 1980s, the frequent profitable unsubsidised Western Ferries operation had captured some 70 per cent of the car traffic, notwithstanding subsidised competition from the new custom-made CalMac vessels. In 1982, after protracted negotiations, the Scottish Office decided that CalMac could continue operation between Dunoon and Gourock, but restricted to an hourly basis with passengers and cars, and that only the passenger element would be subsidised. In fact there is no way of separating the subsidy as between cars and passengers. In any event, had a half-hourly service been sanctioned, the subsidy required by CalMac on the route would have had to be increased by an estimated 50 per cent.

Western Ferries now carries over 85 per cent of the Cowal vehicular traffic and two thirds of the passenger traffic and, after a comprehensive fleet replacement programme, utilising four up-to-date economical vessels, of which two have capacity for 37 cars and two for 45 cars. These give a 15-minute frequency at peak times with operation to midnight at weekends. It is telling that the four Western Ferries vessels' collective fuel consumption is equivalent to that of the single 'streaker' – about 400 litres per hour. In other respects, the relative performance of the competing services is as tabulated in Appendix 1.

The company provides a 24-hour call-out service for ambulances carrying emergency cases – a quality of service unknown elsewhere on the Clyde or in the West Highlands. In 2007 the car marshalling areas were enlarged and second link-spans at both Hunter's Quay and McInroy's Point were installed. Bearing in mind the superior level of service provided by Western Ferries at no cost to the public purse, it is difficult to see how the current subsidised CalMac vehicle ferry service can be justified, considering the longer and subsidised loss-making passage between Dunoon and Gourock, where average carryings have been around eight vehicles per crossing, but to date it continues.

Gourock–Dunoon was not included in the recent tendering of CalMac routes. A separate invitation to tender was issued on the basis that the route would not be subsidized, but no potential operator was forthcoming. At time of writing, CalMac continues to operate the route as a vehicle ferry service, supplemented at morning and evening peaks by the small passenger vessel *Ali Cat*. To cover losses, a subsidy of £2.4 million (2006) was paid, although this was not covered by any tendering process. It has been suggested that this operation is not only grossly unfair, but abstracts earnings of over £1 million (vehicle-borne traffic) from a commercial concern (Western Ferries) and wastes public funds. These points were made to the European Commission.

On the other hand, it could make sense to maintain a direct *passenger* connection with the Gourock rail head as a public transport operation. Indeed, an opportunity exists to create a new high-quality service using fast passenger craft at relatively little cost to the public purse. With this in mind Scottish Enterprise and HIE commissioned Napier University's Transport Research Unit in 2000 to look at options for high-speed passenger ferry services on the Firth of Clyde. The report *Firth of Clyde High-Speed Passenger Ferry Services* revealed that such fast 28-knot passenger craft of about 2 MW power could give a Gourock–Dunoon passage in under ten minutes – half the current timing.

In contrast to the current CalMac vehicle ferry's crew of ten, the fast craft would have a crew of three and about half the fuel consumption per passage, leading to a very substantial saving in operating cost. At current traffic levels, assuming all CalMac cars, drivers and car-borne passengers were diverted to Western Ferries, this would leave some 450,000 foot passengers to be conveyed per annum on the fast craft. On that basis, assuming current fare levels, the subsidy required would be of the order of £800,000 per annum (less if a second-hand vessel were purchased). Since the current (2006) subsidy is £2.4 million this would save £1.6 million in the CalMac subsidy while increasing the Western Ferries profit by £1 million, making a total financial improvement of £2.6 million.

Moreover, the introduction of such an improved quality of service in terms of speed and frequency offers potential to grow the market and so to further reduce the subsidy requirement. It should be noted that the average eight vehicles each way per hour on the current CalMac service would be readily absorbed by Western Ferries without any material increase in costs.

There is a vociferous lobby in Dunoon pledged to maintain the 'CalMac' vehicle ferry, despite its now being effectively superseded by a more efficient alternative. To allay fears of a private operator raising fares disproportionately once subsidised competition is removed, it is understood that Western Ferries would be willing to enter into a fares agreement to contain fares and charges.

A new terminal was constructed at Dunoon at considerable

public expense to enable vehicle ferry end-loading. This has never been used for any regular service and may now be regarded as surplus to requirements and another example of misjudged 'investment' by the former Scottish Executive–CalMac cabal.

Towards the end of 2009, the European Commission issued its decision on the question of subsidies to CalMac and North-Link. The report considered the issues in some depth and it was essentially a legal ruling, which stated that the state aid granted to CalMac for the operation of the Gourock–Dunoon route was incompatible with Article 86(2) of the Treaty. It was, however, further stated that a new open, transparent and non-discriminatory public tender for a passenger-only public service contract along lines set out in the document would be accept-able. It was also indicated that such a service could convey vehicles on a 'commercial basis' so long as this function was separately accounted for to prevent cross-subsidisation. In response, the Scottish Government announced that it proposed to issue such a tender for the route.

The Commission's conclusion is, of course, purely one of legal principle that does not address the issue of value for money to the Scottish taxpayer.

16

UPWARDLY SPIRALLING SUBSIDY

While Western Ferries and Pentland Ferries have been able to capitalise, operate and grow their businesses on a wholly profitable and unsubsidised basis, the same cannot be said about CalMac. In fact, as mentioned earlier, the original ambition was that Caledonian MacBrayne would operate as a commercial concern, covering its costs from revenue, but this proved long ago to be a lost cause.

Until recently, the services operated by Caledonian MacBrayne were subsidised within the terms of the 'undertaking' between the company and the Secretary of State for Scotland. The undertaking listed the routes that the company should operate, but there was no specification as to schedules or fares and little real control was exercised by ministers. In essence, the company submitted an estimate of the likely overall loss for the year and after discussion a grant of or close to that figure was paid by the Scottish Office to the company. The undertaking was not subject to competitive tender and there was little incentive to innovate or improve productivity. It seemed almost as though the company existed to squeeze just a little more money out of the government from one year to the next.

Scotland does not compare favourably with other statesubsidised ferry systems worldwide. Subsidy levels as a proportion of operating costs rose, in the case of CalMac, from 18 per cent in 1991 to 45 per cent in 2007, yet fares and charges remained relatively high and traffic growth is sluggish. For NorthLink, the comparable percentages are 22 per cent in 1991 to an astonishing 62 per cent in 2007. The total subsidy for

CalMac and NothLink in 2007 was £43 million and £31 million respectively. By the 2008–09 Annual Report the reported subsidy had risen to almost £90 million.

An important contributory factor to this state of affairs is that even many of the newer vessels employed are of old-fashioned design, expensive to operate and otherwise less than ideal for their purpose. There is a school of thought too that the routes themselves constrain traffic growth because they are not best selected to maximise, in a cost-effective manner, benefit to many of the island and peninsular communities served.

THE TENDERING DEBACLE

In chapter 9, 'NorthLink', the crass inequity, inefficiency and extravagance of the process whereby the 'Northern Isles' ferry services were tendered is described in some detail. Caledonian MacBrayne's tendering processes were no less shambolic.

The need to comply with European law on state aids to maritime transport required the operation of all state-subsidised ferry routes (or groups of routes) to be open to public tender and subject to Public Service Obligations (PSOs). In 2000, to address this requirement, the then Scottish Executive issued its consultation document – *Delivering Lifeline Ferry Services: A Consultation Paper on Meeting European Union Requirements*. It was assumed by many that individual routes or bundles of routes would each be tendered separately but, after an intensively orchestrated campaign by CalMac and negotiation with the European Commission, it was agreed that the entire CalMac network, except for Gourock–Dunoon, would be tendered as a single bundle. One argument presented in support of this approach was that it was easier for one large fleet to make provision for vessel substitution to cover annual overhauls, breakdowns and the like. This argument ignored the fact that the CalMac fleet is composed of at least two distinct types of vessel, which have no mutual associated terminal, booking and crewing arrangements.

In the event, after years of deliberation, tendering the single bundle was proceeded with. In essence the tender specification required bidders to operate the current routes to the current schedules with the current ships using the same crews under the same terms and conditions and applying the same scale of charges. The opportunity for innovation was virtually eliminated. In view of the relatively short tender period, the ships and terminals formerly owned by CalMac were transferred to a new asset owning company (CMAL) who would then lease these assets back to the successful winner of the tender. As part of this restructuring process the old dormant David MacBrayne Ltd was revived as a group holding company with the following operating subsidiaries: CalMac Ferries Ltd (operating on the Clyde and Hebrides); NorthLink Ferries Ltd (Orkney and Shetland); Cowal Ferries Ltd (Gourock–Dunoon); and Rathlin Ferries Ltd (now dormant, formerly operating to/from Rathin). It also has personnel services: David MacBrayne HR (UK) Ltd; Caledonian MacBrayne Crewing (Guernsey) Ltd; and North-Link Crewing (Guernsey) Ltd.

The tender process was so complex and expensive to comply with, however, that only CalMac, whose very substantial costs in preparing their bid were met by the Scottish Executive (now Government), was able to tackle the process. No other interested party felt able to proceed with making a formal bid. There was indeed a question as to whether the subsidising of bid preparation of the state-owned bidder, but not other private sector bidders, is in itself a breach of state aid rules. On taking over the reins of power in 2007, the new SNP administration had little option but to complete the flawed but already protracted tender process and needless to say, in the absence of any other bidder, CalMac got the job. As may be expected, penalties are payable by the operator for missing performance targets such as punctuality. A private sector operator would have to fund such penalties from its own resources, whereas state-owned CalMac would be in the absurd position of paying penalties to its owner, the state, who would then be forced to make good any losses, should CalMac's operation fail to cover its costs.

The upshot of all this has been a huge additional expense in terms of public funds, with no real improvement in performance and little or no incentive to innovate.

WHY IS SCOTTISH FERRY POLICY IN SUCH A MESS?

When David MacBrayne and the Caledonian Steam Packet Company were merged in 1973 to form Caledonian MacBrayne, two contrasting management and operating styles were brought into a collision course. David MacBrayne may be characterised as old-fashioned but open; the CSPCo well connected but secretive. In reality the merger was effectively a takeover by the CSPCo with the new organisation based at CSPCo's head office at Gourock. The merger must at first have been difficult to weld into a coherent whole, with differing union agreements and operating practices. In time, however, with the introduction of RO-RO and amalgamation of unions, a more coherent structure emerged as monopoly provider of west coast ferry services. An ongoing complaint was that while the company was in receipt of ever-growing subsidies, it had refused to reveal route by route operating costs and revenues.

Subsidised state monopolies have little incentive to improve performance through efficiency gains and as already described, the 'undertaking' with the state seemed to function almost as an open cheque book for the conveyance of taxpayers' funds to the company, with little hard negotiating. Under previous administrations government ministers came and went, many with little understanding of or interest in maritime matters. It therefore fell largely to civil servants to handle the relationship between the state and CalMac and its associate NorthLink. It is perhaps not surprising that a close, some have said 'cosy', relationship developed between them. CalMac was regarded as the 'expert' and the tendency was for the civil service to defer to and promote CalMac's view if alternatives were mooted from outwith the magic circle. Indeed, several of those who have suggested alternative solutions have felt they have been branded ill-informed troublemakers who 'rock the boat' and are not to be trusted, and are discriminated against as a result.

Of course, it is axiomatic that monopolies also abhor competition and Western Ferries' pioneering and efficient operating methods were an uncomfortable reminder that more cost-effective ways of doing things existed. Such has been the discomfort that, rather than embrace innovative operators, public money has been used to 'see off' competitors by under-cutting fares and other measures. On occasion, this unfair practice has worked, but fortunately, despite such interventions, Western Ferries and Pentland Ferries have survived and introduced innovative new solutions to provide enhanced levels of service to their communities.

As stated earlier, the European Commission issued its findings on subsidies to CalMac and NorthLink towards the end of 2009. It concluded that the state aid granted to CalMac and NorthLink for the provision of ferry services is compatible with EU law. In other words the tendering process was legal. The Commission, however, made the following important point: 'In assessing compatibility with Article 86(2) of the Treaty, it is not the Commission's task to check whether the public service could have been delivered more efficiently.'

Therein lies the nub of the problem. The present system is shown to be within the law, but there is a huge question over its fairness, its efficiency and its effectiveness in stimulating the economic and social well-being of our island communities.

In summary, the problem with the state funded ferry sector can be boiled down to the following: we inherit a vicious circle of inertia, because current ship design, route configuration and operating methods are inefficient; an inflexible tender system maintains inefficiency and inhibits innovation; the private sector has skills and ideas, but is prevented from entering the market by a close relationship between civil servants and operators such that subsidised competition is designed to 'see off' competitors.

The result: high cost and poor performance.

Thus from its erstwhile predominance in the world of maritime development, Scotland has now sadly been left far behind. For several decades now, once-innovative designs have become more or less standard among predominantly private-sector ferry operators in much of Europe, Australasia and elsewhere, but not in Scotland, except by our own unsubsidised private operators.

By 2008 there was a growing feeling that the situation had to change, prompting the Scottish Government's root and branch review of ferry services.

17

MORE STRIFE

From the time they had been acquired by Pentland Ferries, *Pentalina B* and *Claymore* had retained the black hull, white superstructure and red funnels of their former owners CalMac. The first visible clue that something new was afoot was the emergence of *Claymore* from her refit for the 2008 season sporting a bright red hull.

The spring of 2008 saw a number of the problems with Scotland's ferry services being aired in the press as the Scottish Parliament's Transport, Infrastructure and Climate Change Committee inquiry into ferry services got underway. As far as Pentland Ferries was concerned, the most fundamental bone of contention remained the grossly unfair situation whereby unsubsidised private operators, namely Pentland Ferries and Western Ferries, were being systematically undermined by subsidised public-sector competition.

The visit by European Transport Commissioner and Vice President Jacques Barrot at the end of April to look at the issue gave some hope that a more equitable approach to supporting Scottish ferry services might emerge. Andrew Banks met with the commissioner in Edinburgh and for the first time was able to show on the map how the Pentland Ferries and NorthLink services ran parallel services between Orkney and Caithness, but that the former got no support at all from the state while the latter attracted an annual operating subsidy, now suggested by some officials to be not far short of a staggering £10 million for that one route alone or some £70.00 for each passenger carried. Apparently this was the first time such a graphic demonstration of the inequity of this 'state aid' issue had been demonstrated. Andrew's face-to-face meeting with Jacques Barrot was reinforced and expanded by written evidence provided by the Gills Bay Harbour Committee and by the author of this book.

MORE SUBSIDISED COMPETITION

One might have assumed that NorthLink would have wished to keep its head down at this point, but no. Incredibly NorthLink announced in April that it was extending its 'Islander Discount' scheme to non-residents of Orkney by inviting every registered island resident to list six unrelated non-islanders as 'families and friends' so that they could enjoy the same 30 per cent discount on the Stromness–Scrabster service, as had been previously available only to Orkney residents. While NorthLink's costs for this were again met from the public purse, Pentland Ferries was denied any such funding to implement a similar scheme on its service. Naturally Pentland Ferries complained to the Scottish Government about this unfair practice but was informed that under the terms of the contract, NorthLink was entitled to retain some £800,000 of 'profit' which they could use as they thought fit, even if it had the effect of undermining another operator.

Another issue that emerged at that time concerned livestock transport from Orkney. By this time, Pentland Ferries carried around 80 per cent of Orkney agriculture's live sheep/lamb exports. It was known that the public purse was funding new twin-deck livestock containers or 'cassettes' for NorthLink. NorthLink now stated publicly that it planned to use these on its Kirkwall (Orkney) to Aberdeen service, a route of more than 100 miles. What concerned those who sought fair play were reports that NorthLink planned to undercut Pentland Ferries' commercial tariffs for livestock trailers, by carrying cattle (at a subsidised price) on the lower deck of these 'cassettes', with sheep carried on the upper decks, if not for free, at least at a much lower rate than the commercial one charged by Pentland Ferries for its 15-mile trip across the Pentland Firth. This matter was also raised with Jacques Barrot.

It was speculated that these moves by NorthLink were part of a twofold bid, on the one hand to undermine the success of Pentland Ferries' new catamaran when it entered service and secondly to fudge and strengthen the case for yet more subsidy to compensate for loss of traffic to Pentland Ferries and to cover (temporarily) higher fuel costs. Again, Pentland Ferries had to bear the increased fuel costs from its own income.

The fuel issue emerged in the spring and summer of 2008 when world oil prices rocketed and NorthLink sought additional subsidy to compensate. To help reduce costs *Hamnavoe*, with her voracious fuel consumption, switched to cheaper but dirtier sulphur fuels which exacerbated her already serious emissions problem. By the autumn the fuel price declined again steeply but it is not clear whether or not an adjustment in subsidy *downwards* was volunteered by NorthLink.

THE NEW SHIP IS LAUNCHED

Meanwhile on the other side of the world at the Balamban yard of FBMA Marine Inc. in Cebu work progressed on the new catamaran. Andrew made periodic visits to the yard to check that work was satisfactory and on target, which by and large it seemed to be. By November 2007 the main structure was almost complete and work had started on the fixtures and fittings, and as 2007 turned to 2008, the form of the vessel became manifest – a sleek and purposeful form hitherto unknown in Scottish waters.

By April she was painted and the colour scheme was no less spectacular. The dramatic effect was emphasised by a bright red hull above a blue bottom and thin white waterline. The red was broken on each side by a broad white diagonal 'chine slash' acting as counterpoint to the pronounced ram bows. The superstructure was brilliant white, relieved by two broad horizontal red bars. The twin white exhaust stacks were emblazoned with the Pentland Ferries curly dragonhead logo. This would surely be an eye-opener to the Scottish travelling public – a leap in style from the nineteenth century to the twenty-first!

Then towards the end of April 2008, the Banks family flew to the Philippines via Hong Kong for a week to set their new baby afloat. Inevitably, the best laid plans 'gang aft agley'. The launch had to be postponed by three days. Nevertheless, on 22 April in a blistering 40C Susan officially named the new vessel *Pentalina* (the favourite time-honoured Banks family appellation), then Susan and Andrew cut the ribbon simultaneously to release a bottle of Orkney wine to christen the brand new multi-million-pound catamaran. The bottle broke first time.

The family took off to enjoy the facilities of a resort but returned to Cebu on Friday 25 April for the long-awaited launch. Susan, suitably attired in smart casual black and white tropical garb, was, to her chagrin, given a yellow hard hat which according to daughter Jenni gave her the appearance of a policewoman. Policewoman or not, at around 1 p.m. Philippine time *Pentalina* at last slipped into her natural element.

It was expected that sea trials could take place more or less immediately and that *Pentalina* would be formally handed over in the middle of the month. Thereafter she would be able to undertake the delivery voyage from the Philippines to Orkney under her own power to replace *Claymore* on the St Margaret's Hope–Gills Bay route in June, in time for the summer season. Unfortunately this was not to be.

HOLD-UPS AND FRUSTRATION

BBC News reported on 4 May the commencement of six weeks of sea trials, but when Andrew returned to Cebu at the end of May with a crew to bring the ferry home they were horrified to discover that work on the ship wasn't complete. FBMA Marine blamed the hold-ups on delays in the delivery of materials from suppliers. Among important items still to be delivered were life rafts and rescue boat, without which the ship could of course not proceed to sea. It also emerged that key technical staff had left the yard for other employment.

Nearly a month later, on 24 June, BBC News reported: 'A catamaran ferry for the Caithness to Orkney route, which was due to arrive in Scotland last month, is still at a shipyard in the Philippines.'

It wasn't until a further month later, on 25 July, that *Orkney Today* was able to report that sea trials had gone better than expected and that the new multi-million-pound ferry *Pentalina* was at last ready to set sail from the Philippines. The report revealed that the departure would end the considerable delay in her construction which had cost Pentland Ferries boss Andrew Banks some of his lucrative summer season trade. Besides the additional cost of maintaining a crew in the Philippines when they should have been undertaking the delivery voyage, *Claymore* was meanwhile running at full capacity and having to turn valuable customers away, thereby depriving the company of revenue. In fact, during the sea trials the hydraulic pumps that activated the bow thrusters packed up and as the yard could not remedy this defect in time, Andrew decided to leave Cebu without working bow thrusters.

In light of the financial loss he had incurred through the ferry's late delivery, Andrew announced that he would be consulting solicitors about a possible claim against the ship-building firm. A partially satisfactory financial accommodation was agreed, however, avoiding expensive and time-consuming litigation.

18

THE DELIVERY VOYAGE
FROM HELL

At last on the morning of Friday, 26 July, under the command of Orcadian Captain Willie Pottinger and with Andrew Banks on board, *Pentalina* set out from Cebu in fair weather on her 10,000-mile, four-week voyage via a series of former strategic outposts of the British Empire to her new home in Orkney. The eight-man complement settled in for what they hoped would be a straightforward passage. Of course, besides transferring the vessel from her birthplace to her new home, the delivery voyage was seen as a shakedown cruise to test the vessel's systems and identify any problems. Before the passage would be completed there would be problems galore and systems and nerves would be tested to the limit.

On the second day out, crossing the Sulu Sea, a force-eight gale blew up, with the ship encountering heavy beam seas, not unlike conditions on a bad day in the Pentland Firth. *Pentalina* coped with these conditions fully up to expectations and after passing through the Balabac Strait the course was west-south-west through the South China Sea to the great entrepot of Singapore, where she arrived on 31 July. Singapore is the world's busiest port, handling annually over a billion gross tons of shipping, and 23 million TEUs (20-foot equivalent units) of containerised traffic, of which a high proportion is 'transipped'. Singapore is also the world's biggest ship refuelling centre and as *Pentalina* took on fuel and fresh water Andrew left his new ship to fly back to Orkney.

As Andrew winged his way home, a replenished *Pentalina* left

Singapore, heading north-west through the Strait of Malacca. This infamous strait between Indonesia and Malaysia has long been a haven for pirates and terrorists. These are far removed from the colourful swashbuckling characters of Hollywood. They are ruthless armed criminals who think nothing of firing rocket-propelled grenades at vessels to force them to stop. Every year seamen are killed or go missing following pirate attacks. This menace has been enough to spur the Indonesian, Malay and Singaporean navies into jointly patrolling the Straits, but this has not as yet wholly removed the threat. Captain Pottinger ordered 'lockdown', that is all external doors were locked along with all cabin doors, as a precaution against pirates or terrorists attacking the ship. Fortunately there was no such problem and *Pentalina* rounded the northern tip of Sumatra to head due west across the Indian Ocean, arriving on 8 August at Galle, Sri Lanka, the next fuel stop.

Galle, a UNESCO declared World Heritage Site and a city with a colourful history, is the capital of Sri Lanka's southern province. It has a magnificent fort, built by the Dutch, and was Sri Lanka's earliest European administrative centre, the major port and largest city in the country until the British shifted their focus to Colombo, about 70 miles to the north. In 1815, under the terms of the Kandian Convention, the British gained control of the entire island (then called Ceylon).

As soon as bunkering was complete, *Pentalina* left Galle astern, heading westward between the Maldive and Laccadive Islands and across the Arabian Sea towards Aden in the Yemen, another former British possession – a passage expected to take seven days, subject to good weather. In the event *Pentalina*'s sea-going capability was again tested by a south-easterly gale and 8-metre swells in the Indian Ocean and once more she coped admirably. It was not the sea conditions that were to precipitate trouble, but trouble of another kind. There appeared to be a major problem with the generators and the ship's main engines, threatening a total loss of power and steering. There was no option but to make for the nearest safe haven, the port of Salalah in Oman, where she arrived on 16 August.

THE DIESEL BUG

A series of cryptic announcements appeared in the local press from time to time, explaining unforeseen delays and expressing the hope that it would not be long before *Pentalina* was on her way again. On 24 August *Pentalina* was 'awaiting Caterpillar service following generator problems crossing from Sri Lanka'. After a number of further announcements, the *John O'Groat Journal* mentioned on 12 September that *Pentalina* remained in Salalah because her fuel filters had picked up 'the diesel bug' due to water in the fuel.

So what is the diesel bug? It is, in short, bacteria contamination of diesel fuel. A diesel engine needs two essential supplies: air with an adequate oxygen content, and clean, uncontaminated fuel. If a vessel has been subject to variations in weather and temperature, or fuel has been stored for anything longer than a few months, there is a danger of contamination. The most common contaminant is water, usually building up from condensation. Diesel is an organic fuel so, when water is present in diesel fuel, bacteria are able to breed. This 'bug' will form a layer between the fuel and the water and as it breeds it produces waste, which usually takes the form of dark lumps.

Water can also encourage the build-up of microbes, algae and even fungi, which can develop many types of sludge and residue within the fuel. This biomass may drop to the bottom of the tank or it may be suspended in the fuel. Either way, it clogs up the filters and can lead to expensive damage to equipment, with breakdowns in power supply. A single cell, weighing only one millionth of a gram, can grow to a biomass of 10 kilograms in just 12 hours, resulting in a biomass several centimetres thick across the fuel/water interface. Once contaminated diesel enters the fuel system, it is very difficult to eradicate. The only cure is to clean the entire system thoroughly with a cleaning agent, and this was done, together with renewal and re-calibration of the engine injectors. A further problem that had contributed to the generator problems was that the return fuel lines had been set too high, thereby inhibiting the flow of fuel to the engines.

UNDER WAY AGAIN AT LAST

It was not until 15 November at 16:00 that *Pentalina* finally cast off from Oman to make her way across the Gulf of Aden and through the Red Sea to the Suez Canal, where she was scheduled to arrive on the 22nd. Having successfully negotiated the pirate-infested waters of the Strait of Malacca in August, a deadly new threat loomed. On that same day the 1,000-foot oil tanker *Sirius Star*, with a cargo of 2 million barrels of Arabian crude oil, hit the headlines. She was hijacked in the Indian Ocean by Somali pirates – the largest vessel ever to be captured by pirates. What next!

Lloyds List of 20 November announced '*Pentalina* passes through pirate waters':

> Extra security measures were taken when the catamaran *Pentalina* finally resumed her delivery voyage from the Philippines to Scotland and passed through 'pirate waters' in the Indian Ocean and Gulf of Aden earlier this week. With tension heightened following seizure of the super-tanker *Sirius Star* and other vessels, there was extra vigilance by the crew of *Pentalina*, which reaches Suez tomorrow (Friday).

Happily, no pirates were encountered, nor was there any recurrence of the fuel and generator problems that had rendered *Pentalina* immobile for so long in Salalah. *Pentalina* passed through the Red Sea to reach Suez as schelduled on the 22nd. She negotiated the Suez Canal without incident to enter the Mediterannean Sea and by 25 November was passing Libya on

her way westwards towards Gibraltar, the next scheduled
bunker stop, where the crew were to change over with a relief
crew. *Pentalina* encountered two days of storm force winds, in
the course of which the base casting for the rescue boat davit
cracked. Had the heavy davit broken free in these wild conditions it could have fallen overboard and pierced the ship's
shell plating or, perhaps worse, fallen inboard and pierced the
deck above the engine space, possibly immobilising the ship
and allowing water ingress. The ship's crew struggled in the
atrocious weather to lash down the precarious davit to prevent
any possibility of such disastrous damage. Thankfully, they
succeeded. The port of Gibraltar was closed because of the
weather but *Pentalina* was able to put into Almeria, some 200
miles east of Gibraltar, on 29 November where she took on fuel.
With the ship in Almeria and the relief crew in Gibraltar, a very
expensive return taxi ride was the only solution.

By 5 December *Pentalina* had passed the Portuguese coast
heading north to the Bay of Biscay. The next scheduled stop
would be her home port of St Margaret's Hope. The final stage
of her marathon 10,000-mile passage took her round Finisterre
and Land's End, through the Irish Sea, round the Mull of
Kintyre, up through the Sound of Jura, the Sound of Mull and
the Sound of Sleat and round Cape Wrath to arrive just after
dawn, finally and safely, in St Margaret's Hope at 08:30 on the
morning of Tuesday, 9 December.

19

MEANWHILE

The whole episode of delays and frustration connected with the building and delivery of *Pentalina* would have tried the patience of a saint, and more seriously had denied Pentland Ferries the opportunity to increase capacity, traffic and revenue on the short sea crossing for the 2008 season. Nevertheless, during that vexed period Andrew was active with a varied assortment of new schemes.

Firstly there were modifications to be made at Gills Bay to accommodate the new ship. A wider area alongside the quay had to be dredged, to provide increased manoeuvring space to allow for the *Pentalina*'s greater beam. At the Hope too, alterations were required. As *Pentalina*'s belting was 700mm higher than *Claymore*'s, the quay deck was too low to make contact in conditions of very high water, so it was necessary to add extended fenders to the quay face to ensure proper contact with the ship's belting at all times.

FISHING IN OTHER WATERS

As has already been mentioned, *Pentalina B* had been engaged intermittently on livestock charters across the English Channel, but Andrew was looking for other opportunities for expanding the business.

At the end of July 2008, Pentland Ferries' plans to revive a ferry service across the Forth between Burntisland and Granton on a commercial basis were unveiled. The scheme was for a 30-minute crossing carrying up to 300 passengers at a time, subject to public cash to build waiting rooms and landing facilities for the boats. Pentland Ferries proposed to employ two high-speed passenger catamarans that were available for sale at the time. Fife Council confirmed interest in launching a ferry link across the Forth but indicated that it had been approached by a number of businesses who had expressed a desire to operate some kind of Forth ferry and were unwilling to commit themselves to any particular operator.

Andrew was all too aware that once *Pentalina* was eventually in operation on the St Margaret's Hope–Gills Bay station, he would have to find employment for *Claymore*. The most obvious potential lay in the west, where two opportunities seemed to lie. These were: reviving the crossing between Campbeltown (Kintyre) and Ballycastle in Northern Ireland, and providing a service between Lochboisdale (South Uist) and Mallaig.

A summer-only service between Campbeltown and Bally-castle had been operated for a few years in the late 1990s by the Argyll and Antrim Steam Packet Company, a subsidiary of the Sea Containers group, but after the subsidy ceased, the service was withdrawn. The ship employed had been none other than *Claymore*. One of the key beneficiaries of the link was Campbel-town, which was at the end of a long peninsula and, as a consequence, well off the main tourist routes. Since the demise of the Argyll and Antrim service, there had existed a local campaign to reinstate the route and the previous Scottish Executive had indicated that a subsidy could be available.

Andrew Banks threw his hat into the ring and after discussion with local interests suggested also that the operation could include a link between Campbeltown and Ayrshire. Negotia-tions and local meetings took place off and on, and in September the Minister for Transport, Infrastructure and Climate Change (Stewart Stevenson) announced that consultants had been commissioned by the Scottish Government and the Northern Ireland Executive to undertake a Scottish Transport Appraisal Guidance (STAG) of the proposed service and that once it was available, ministers in Scotland and Northern Ireland would consider the costs and benefits of the proposed service and reach a decision about the way forward.

There was also a history regarding a service between Lochboisdale and Mallaig. The ferry links between South Uist and the Scottish mainland were either via Oban, a long and time-consuming passage, or by the shorter sea route via North Uist and Uig in Skye, which presented a longer road journey. The prospect of Mallaig as an alternative landfall, at around three hours' passage by conventional ferry, was a convenient compromise and had found much support in Uist for a number of years, culminating in close to 2,000 signing a petition campaigning for the link. CalMac had been asked to look at it as an option but had been unable or unwilling to come up with a workable solution.

Again, indicating that he could operate the route with *Claymore*, Andrew opened up discussion with community landlords Stòras Uibhist, who were among the main advocates of the Mallaig route provided that a £1 million subsidy, that had apparently been offered previously, was still available. It had previously been assumed that any service connecting Lochboisdale and Mallaig would be provided by CalMac. Concerns were raised over the impact any new service might have on the route between Barra and Oban, but it was pointed out that agreement with Pentland Ferries would allay these fears. Introducing the *Claymore* on the Lochboisdale–Mallaig route would free up capacity on *Lord of the Isles* to improve services to Barra, as well as other islands served from Oban. Anyway, the proposal was put to ministers.

This new initiative would of course break CalMac's long standing monopoly of the islands' main sea crossings, a circumstance that was highly desirable, but anathema to the CalMac board, who reportedly lobbied hard to frustrate the Pentland Ferries initiative. In August the *West Highland Free Press* and *Stornoway Gazette* reported that the Scottish Government had announced that the proposed arrangement would have to be put out to a fresh round of tendering, thereby stalling the whole process. It was further stated that a meeting with Stòras Uibhist would take place in September involving CalMac, who could not find a way of operating the service (other than by building a new £25 million vessel), but not involving Pentland Ferries, who could (using *Claymore*, which had originally been built for the Lochboisdale route and which carried the necessary Class IIA certificate) – an extraordinary state of affairs. Again the fates, or more precisely vested interests, seemed to conspire against another cost-effective, practical proposal by Pentland Ferries.

A LIFESAVER

It does not need the intellect of a Harvard business professor to guess that the costs incurred by Pentland Ferries by the delayed delivery of the new catamaran and the loss of revenue due to her non-participation in the 2008 summer season seriously under-mined the company's cash position. Indeed, NorthLink personnel had been heard to spread the word, with just a whiff of unconcealed *Schadenfreude*, that Andrew was in serious trouble financially. Then at that nadir in the company's affairs came an unexpected but very welcome windfall.

In November the link-span at Ullapool used by the CalMac Stornoway ferry was scheduled for replacement which meant that it was to be out of action for a period as a means of loading and discharging vehicles. To provide an alternative vehicle carrying service to Stornoway for that period, *Pentalina B* was chartered by CalMac to run as a freighter between Stornoway and Uig in Skye. The charter fee for *Pentalina B* represented a vital injection of cash to the business in its hour of need.

AND ON THE PENTLAND FIRTH

With the non-arrival of *Pentalina*, *Claymore* soldiered on as before between St Margaret's Hope and Gills Bay, with record carryings at the peak of the season. There were occasional interruptions. *Claymore* was off service for part of Monday, 25 August 2008, because of the funeral of a crew member who was tragically drowned in a boating accident while off duty at St Margaret's Hope the previous week. In the circumstances, the 08:00 sailing from St Margaret's Hope and the 09:45 from Gills Bay were rescheduled to depart half an hour earlier. The 12:00 from St Margaret's Hope and the 13:45 from Gills Bay were cancelled, after which the 18:00 from St Margaret's Hope and 19:45 from Gills Bay ran as normal.

Pentland Ferries was not the only ferry operator to be affected by occasional unforeseen circumstances. On 1 October BBC Good Morning Scotland announced that NorthLink sailings that morning and afternoon were cancelled because one of *Hamnavoe*'s stabilisers would not retract. This defect had prevented her from berthing at Scrabster on her first sailing, as a result of which she had to return to Stromness without landing her passengers and vehicles.

CHRISTMAS REUNION

With the late arrival of *Pentalina* from her delivery voyage and the need for her to undergo final fitting out, testing and security clearance after her arrival at St Margaret's Hope, coupled with the necessity for *Claymore* to proceed to dry dock, all sailings were withdrawn from 2 to 22 December. *Pentalina B* arrived in St Margaret's Hope on the night of Monday the 22nd and was put back into her old route between Gills Bay and St Margaret's Hope on Tuesday the 23rd to cover sailings from 08:00, but limited to 12 passengers only. *Claymore* arrived back from dry-dock on the following morning (Christmas Eve in fact) around 11:00, taking over from the *Pentalina B* on the 17:00 sailing.

For the first and last time, all three of the Pentland Ferries fleet were berthed in St Margaret's Hope over Christmas and Hogmanay: old stager *Pentalina B* berthed alongside new girl *Pentalina*, with trusty *Claymore* on station to maintain the service until *Pentalina* was cleared for action. And so as the midnight bells rang out 2008, a sigh of relief emanated from *Ceol na Mara*, the Banks's home at St Margaret's Hope. It had been a hard, hard year but now, at last, hopefully the means were in place to show how Scottish ferries should be run.

20

NOT QUITE THERE YET

With *Pentalina* in Orkney at last, Andrew could now sort out a number of matters that had to be attended to before the new ship could enter service. The flooring that had been warped as a result of long exposure to excessive heat in the Middle East had to be re-laid. One of the vital tasks in the New Year, however, was to hire a crane to swap over *Claymore*'s rescue boat davit for *Pentalina*'s. Then on 6 January 2009 *Pentalina* left St Margaret's Hope for the MCA inspection required for granting of the passenger certificate and security clearance. This was a thorough evaluation which necessitated a full evacuation procedure and the inflation of life rafts. The life rafts had then to be sent away for repacking. A list of relatively minor defects for correction was issued and *Pentalina* returned to the Hope. The required adjustments were quickly effected and the final MCA inspection was scheduled. That day the airport was closed due to snow and the Aberdeen surveyor was unable to reach Orkney. As it happened, another MCA inspector had been stranded in Orkney and in the end he was able to carry out the inspection. By 7 p.m. that evening *Pentalina* was awarded her passenger certificate, allowing her to carry up to 250 passengers with a minimum crew of eight. In normal operation a purser and steward were also to be carried, bringing the crewing to ten – one third of *Hamanvoe*'s minimum complement of 29! Subject to installation of canopies on the sun deck, the MCA had agreed an increase in the passenger certificate to 350 without further increase in crew numbers.

On Friday, 30 January 2009, in the presence of a Radio

Orkney reporter, the sleek new catamaran loaded and departed from St Margaret's Hope at 8 a.m. on her first scheduled passage. As she set off, the skipper lost steering, circled and returned to the pier. Someone had left a valve open. This was quickly rectified and once more *Pentalina* departed, this time successfully. As she approached Gills Bay, however, the starboard engines and bow thrusters (long since fitted) lost power. After four attempts *Pentalina* berthed at Gills Bay. The southbound vehicles and passengers were landed and the northbound traffic loaded and the return passage was accomplished successfully. With the wind increasing, the captain decided to make no more trips until the engine and thrusters problem was resolved.

The threefold problem stemmed from the misaligned fuel lines that had been diagnosed at Salalah, hydraulic pumps that were insufficiently robust and an absence of clutches between main inboard engines and thruster pumps – all, it seems, the result of faulty or badly chosen installation back in Cebu. Resolving these problems by specialists was to take time.

Trusty *Claymore* was brought back into service. As she had sacrificed her rescue boat davit to *Pentalina*, she was restricted to 12 passengers and in this constrained condition she maintained the route through February to mid March when the 12-passenger restriction was lifted and her passenger certificate restored. Meantime, Andrew had put *Claymore* on the market and got an excellent offer from a Danish company. The offer was accepted. Then a Fijian company expressed an interest in *Pentalina B*, which if taken up would have allowed her to join her erstwhile CalMac stablemate, former Stornoway ferry *Suilven*, to take up a new life in the South Pacific. This deal, however, fell through.

The race was now on to get *Pentalina* into reliable operating form before *Claymore* left for Denmark. It was not until 24 March that installation of the substitute hydraulic equipment was completed, although the facility to de-clutch the hydraulic pumps while under way could not be accomplished in time.

Over the following two days the bow thrusters were tested and on 27 March BBC's Good Morning Scotland news programme announced that *Pentalina*'s bow thrusters had functioned successfully and that, weather permitting, the new catamaran would take up her station that evening. However, that Friday and Saturday bad weather had disrupted ferry sailings throughout Scotland and it was felt best to wait until conditions improved before inaugurating sailings. At long last, at five o'clock on Sunday 30th and without ceremony, *Pentalina* commenced operation on the route for which she had been designed, and just in time for the spring school holiday rush. She performed fully up to expectation.

21

A NEW DAWN

For months prospective telephone enquirers had asked, 'Is the new boat in service yet?', only to be disappointed. Now the answer was 'YES!' In the first few weeks of April the weather had been mixed, but while numerous ferry sailings were cancelled elsewhere in Scotland, *Pentalina* coped well and no Pentland Ferries sailings were cancelled. *Pentalina*'s carryings soared and that brought in much-needed revenue.

Cash flow was further enhanced by events in the far south-west of Scotland. The Islay ferry *Isle of Arran* had to be taken off station for repairs and *Pentalina B* was chartered by CalMac for the month of April to provide additional cover on the station for which she had originally been designed, 40 years before. On Saturday, 4 April, *Claymore* set off for Denmark but had to return because of engine trouble. It seems that during *Claymore*'s last dry-docking in Aberdeen, the aluminium rim of a safety lamp had been dropped into the sump of the starboard engine. It had sloshed around there unsuspected for over three months and finally as *Claymore* had set off for Denmark had attached itself to the suction pipe, thereby blocking it. That it had not happened while on service before *Pentalina* was available suggested that fortune was indeed now favouring Andrew Banks. The offending item was duly removed and at around 8 p.m. on the evening of 8 April *Claymore* set off again for delivery to her new owners in Denmark.

Clearly, notwithstanding what is believed to be the world's most heavily subsidised crossing for its distance between Scrabster and Stromness, at something not too far short of £10 million per annum, or almost £3.00 per passenger per mile, NorthLink must still have felt threatened by *Pentalina*. An online advertisement appeared on the Google search engine as follows:

Pentland Ferries
Fast and Frequent Ferries to
Shetland and Orkney – Book Online
www.NorthLinkFerries.co.uk

This deceptive site, purporting to give access to the Pentland Ferries website, in fact led directly to NorthLink's reservations portal, a dirty trick that was unworthy of a publicly owned and funded company, but perhaps in view of past experience, not wholly surprising.

In view of this and the general issue of unfair competition, Andrew took the opportunity to write to Stewart Stevenson (Minister for Transport, Infrastructure and Climate Change), pointing out the existence of the bogus web link and asking advice as to how he might 'level the playing field' by applying for the 'friends and family' subsidy that NorthLink received. He also took the opportunity to invite the minister to visit Pentland Ferries to see and hear at first hand how the service had been developed, whilst offering pointers as to how other Scottish ferry services might be more efficiently operated in the future. In the event the minister was not able to pay a personal visit to Pentland Ferries but it appeared that notice had been taken of at least one issue that had been so troubling to Pentland Ferries. While ministerial contacts with CalMac and NorthLink have been commonplace for many years, this was the first time any government minister or his aides had taken the trouble to pay attention to Andrew's concerns. Within days of this contact the mischievous web link was removed. Perhaps at last the message that Pentland Ferries had something to offer was being taken seriously.

Despite this intervention, however, NorthLink was not dissuaded from other forms of unfair competition. Cheap overnight berths were offered on *Hamnavoe* for passengers taking the early morning sailing, thereby depriving Orkney landladies of trade. It had been generally accepted hitherto that ferry subsidies had been intended to aid the island economy, not to undermine it. More seriously in its impact on Pentland Ferries was a deal apparently struck between NorthLink and the Kirkwall Auction Mart whereby livestock floats were carried free to Orkney and taken back to Scrabster for £200.

Irritating though the unfair subsidised competition has been, the Pentland Ferries operation has multiple advantages over the NorthLink service. *Pentalina*'s capital cost was one quarter that of *Hamnavoe*'s, and she functions with one third the crew and one quarter the fuel consumption per crossing, while the shorter crossing time permits four return crossings on peak summer days. For these reasons, among others, *Pentalina*'s operating cost per crossings is a small fraction that of *Hamnavoe*'s, even before taking account of well over £1 million in berthing dues *Hamnavoe* has to pay at Stromness and Scrabster and massive leasing charges occasioned by the now discredited PPP (public private partnership) arrangement under which the vessel is made available to NorthLink.

In any event, notwithstanding a severe national economic recession, the 2009 summer season was a bumper one for Pentland Ferries. Although freight carryings had been affected somewhat by the NorthLink–Kirkwall Mart deal, traffic was at new record levels overall with an 18 per cent increase in traffic. Indeed, for sailing after sailing *Pentalina* ran at capacity. Despite doubts in some quarters that a catamaran would be suitable for the Pentland Firth crossing, *Pentalina*'s performance fully justified Andrew's faith in this type of vessel.

Pentalina's success must have really spooked the David MacBrayne Group's management, for in the chairman's one and a half page statement in the group's 2008–09 annual report special mention was made of a 'highly respected' 'major' study by Strathclyde University comparing mono-hull and multi-hull (i.e. catamaran) designs which demonstrated 'conclusively' that mono-hulls had superior sea-keeping, comfort and manoeuvrability characteristics. The over-emphatic intensity of the language suggests an element of 'protesting too much', bearing in mind that the conclusions of this theoretical desk study have been seriously challenged and that catamarans of all shapes, sizes and speeds have been in successful and reliable operation worldwide for decades. On the issue of manoeuvrability, *Pentalina*, with her quadruple screws and bow thrusters, actually outclasses most rivals and can turn nimbly in her own length.

It may be instructive to quote from the conclusion of a scathing technical critique of the above study by one naval architect experienced in catamaran design: '. . . So for the consultant who did the analysis for CalMac to conclude that mono-hulls have much better sea-keeping characteristics, we suggest they conduct some credible testing before making such incorrect and foolish statements. We hope CalMac did not waste any taxpayers' money in paying for this.'

One of the crucial points is that, while 'high speed' catamarans are subject to wave height restrictions because of discomfort to passengers, this constraint does not apply to well designed 'medium speed' cats such as *Pentalina*. In fact, not one Pentland Ferries sailing was lost throughout the summer season due to weather (or any other circumstance) and it was not until late September that one trip had to be cancelled due to a very strong westerly swell at Gills Bay – a berthing issue rather than a sea-keeping one. To tackle this one limitation to Pentland Ferries' otherwise first-rate operation, Andrew has been looking at options for further extending the pier at Gills Bay.

So with *Pentalina* now well established to provide a fast, frequent, clean, convenient service, Pentland Ferries can now well and truly be regarded as Orkney's preferred ferry provider. This is well illustrated by looking at each point in turn:

Fast: one hour quicker in overall journey time between Kirkwall and Caithness compared with NorthLink, taking account of drive time to port, check-in time and sea passage.

Clean: less noxious emissions and one quarter of the CO_2 discharge per crossing than *Hamnavoe*. In these times of concern for climate change, emissions by ships are now a major concern.

Frequent: up to four departures daily.

Convenient: simple charging system, no ID required. North-Link requires all passengers to present photo ID before they are permitted to board.

And of course all this at no cost to the taxpayer! All that is now required is due recognition from the authorities that the Pentland Ferries approach is the way forward for Scottish ferry policy.

The reader may ask how it is that country boy Andrew Banks could create a whole new state-of-the-art ferry service in the face of extravagant, heavily subsidised competition backed by teams of influential highly salaried 'experts'. Perhaps the answer is that successful farmers are practical men who have to solve multiple problems as cheaply as possible to survive. They have to learn by their mistakes and learn quickly. 'Experts', as often as not well qualified in theory, may never have got their hands dirty in practice and leave others to live with the consequences and high cost of their mistakes. In this regard senior bankers of the modern sort and nationalised ferry company bosses spring to mind.

22

FAREWELL TO THE HERO

And so with a brand new catamaran ferry in service on Orkney's short sea route, the saga of Andrew Banks is brought up to date. His plans for the future remain to be revealed another day. It is time for us to leave the Banks family to let them get on with the business of developing their company into a model of how Scottish ferries *should* be operated.

We shake hands, take our leave and board *Pentalina* for the return passage across the Firth. We have not completely left the family behind, for Andrew's and Susan's daughter Kathryn is ship's purser. It truly is a family business.

As the last vehicle is taken aboard, it is gratifying to see that the deck is crammed with six trailers and a full complement of cars – a very good sign. Lines are cast off and we proceed to sea, out of the Hope, round Hoxa Head and into Scapa Flow. We ponder the amazing achievement of Andrew and Susan Banks in creating, or perhaps it should be re-creating, the short sea crossing where others have failed. That Andrew did not fail, despite limited financial resources and an almost endless catalogue of setbacks, tribulations and obstructions, deliberately and malevolently placed in his way, is a testament to the man's tenacity. That he has brought into service Scotland's most fuel- and cost-efficient vehicle ferry is a testament to his perspicacity. Ordinary mortals succeed when fortune smiles. The man who succeeds when the odds are stacked against him, when other men try to trip him, when there is no safety net and the future looks black – that man is a hero.

We wish our Pentland Hero good fortune and safe passage in the future.

We go on deck. *Pentalina* is cracking along at 17 knots. She'll make the crossing in under the hour. As we pass Swona to port, the coastline of Caithness lies ahead and the westering sun makes the Pentland Firth sparkle – a good omen, we feel.

BIBLIOGRAPHY

BOOKS

Blue, Arthur, *The Sound of Sense*, Glasgow, undated

Brand, John, *Brief Description of Orkney, Zetland, Pentland Firth and Caithness*, Edinburgh, 1701

Campbell, HF, *Caithness and Sutherland*, Cambridge, 1920

Cleg, Peter V, *A Flying Start to the Day*, Godalming, 1986

Congregational Board of Canisbay Parish Church, edited by Anne Houston, *Lest we Forget: The Parish of Canisbay*, Canisbay, 1996

Cormack, Alastair & Anne, *Days of Orkney Steam*, Kirkwall, 1971

Deayton, Alistair, *Orkney & Shetland Steamers*, Stroud, 2002

Defoe, Daniel, *A Tour through the Whole Island of Great Britain, 1724–6*, London

Donaldson, Gordon, *A Northern Commonwealth*, Edinburgh, 1990

Donaldson, Gordon, *Northwards by Sea*, Edinburgh, 1966

Duckworth, CLD & Langmuir, GEL, *Clyde River & Other Steamers*, Glasgow, 1972

Duckworth, CLD & Langmuir, GEL, *West Highland Steamers*, Prescot, 1967

Gardiner, *Stage Coach to John O'Groats*, London, 1961

Haldane, ARB, *New Ways through the Glens*, Edinburgh, 1962

Haldane, ARB, *Three Centuries of Scottish Posts*, Edinburgh, 1971

Linklater, Eric, *Orkney and Shetland*, London, 1965

Miller, James, *A Wild and Open Sea*, Kirkwall, 1994

Miller, James, *Caithness*, London, 1979

Pálsson, Herman and Edwards, Paul, *Orkneyinga Saga*, London, 1981

Robins, Nick S & Meek, Donald E, *The Kingdom of MacBrayne*, Edinburgh, 2006

Smith, Colin J, *In Fair Weather and in Foul, 30 Years of Scottish Passenger Ships and Ferries*, Narbeth, 1999

Smith, Peter L, *The Naval Wrecks of Scapa Flow*, Kirkwall, 1989

Stevenson Locomotive Society, The, *The Highland Railway company and its Constituents and Successors 1855–1955*, London, 1955

Sutherland, Iain, *Caithness 1770 to 1832*, Wick, 1995

Valance, HA, *The Highland Railway* (revised and extended edition), London, 1963

Wilson, Andrew, *The Sound of Silence, Subsidy and Competition in West Coast Shipping*, Glasgow, undated

Wilson, Andrew, *The Sound of the Clam*, Glasgow, undated

ARTICLES, REPORTS, PAMPHLETS, ETC

Caledonian MacBrayne Annual Reports

Caledonian MacBrayne brochures and timetables

Caledonian Steam Packet Company brochures and timetables

Clyde River Steamer Club Reviews, 1972, 1989, 1997, 1999, 2000, 2001, 2002, 2003, 2004 and 2006

David MacBrayne Annual Report, 2008–2009

David MacBrayne timetables, various

Department of Agriculture and Fisheries for Scotland, *Report of the Highland Transport Board*, Edinburgh, 1967

Financial Times, *Brussels to Probe Scottish Ferry Subsidies*, London, 2008

Hall, Ian, *Western Ferries, Clyde Steamers No. 32*, Summer 1996

Herald, The, various issues

Highlands and Islands Development Board, *A Ferry for Orkney*, Inverness, 1969

Highlands and Islands Development Board, *Occasional Bulletin 6, Highlands and Islands Transport Review*, Inverness, 1975

Highlands and Islands Development Board, *Roads to the Isles – a study of sea freight charges in the Highlands and Islands of Scotland*, Inverness, 1974

HMSO, *Passenger Fares and Freight Charges of the North of Scotland, Orkney and Shetland Shipping Company Limited*, London, 1968

HMSO, *Transport Services in the Highlands and Islands*, London, 1963

John o'Groat Journal, various issues

Liddle, LH, 'Northern "Saints"', *Sea Breezes Magazine*, May and June 1960

Maritime Research Group, Napier University Transport Research Institute, *Future Options for Northern Isles Ferry Services*, Edinburgh, January 2006

MDS Transmodal, Gills Harbour Study, Chester, 1993

Mearns Publications, *Caithness Official Guide*, Aberdeen, undated

Northern Maritime Corridor (NMC) Project Group Report, EU Interreg IIIB, Brussels 2006

NorthLink Ferries brochures

North of Scotland Orkney & Shetland Shipping Co brochures and sailing lists

Orcadian, The, various issues

Orkney County Council and Kirkwall Town Council, *Orkney Official Guide*, undated

P&O Ferries brochures

Pedersen, Roy N, *A Better Way to Run Ferries, Response to the Inquiry into Ferry Services in Scotland*, Inverness, 2008

Pedersen, Roy N, *Ferry Futures*, Inverness, 1999

Pentland Ferries brochures

Press & Journal, various issues

Scotsman, The, various issues

Scottish Transport Annual Reports, various

Shetland News, The, various issues

Stornoway Gazette, various issues

Sunday Herald, various issues

West Highland Free Press, various issues

Western Ferries timetables

APPENDIX 1

STATISTICAL COMPARISONS

PENTLAND FERRIES NEW VESSEL *PENTALINA*
COMPARED WITH *CLAYMORE* AND *HAMNAVOE*

	Pentalina	Claymore	Hamnavoe
Capital cost	£7 million	Written off	£30 million
Length (waterline)	64m	70m	104m
Beam	20m	15.5m	18.6m
Draught	2.5m	3m	4.4m
Crew	10	14	28
Capacity load: cars or equivalent	78 cars	47 cars	95 cars
Service speed	16 knots	13.5 knots	17 knots
Full displacement	1,300 tonnes	1,800 tonnes	5,883 tonnes
Max revenue deadweight	380 tonnes	300 tonnes	1,200 tonnes
Fuel consumption	620 litres/hr	600 litres/hr	1,835 litres/hr
Revenue deadweight as per cent of total displacement	38 per cent	17 per cent	20 per cent

COMPARISON BETWEEN WESTERN FERRIES *SOUND OF JURA* WITH CALMAC *PIONEER*

	Sound of Jura	Pioneer
Length O.A. metres	49	67
Beam metres	11	14
Draught metres	2.44	2.36
Deadweight tonnes	217	245
Speed knots	13.5	16
Vehicle capacity	36	30
Passengers	250	273
Crew	6	21

WESTERN FERRIES AND CALMAC INVERCLYDE–COWAL ROUTES COMPARED

	Western Ferries	CalMac
Crew per vessel	4 or 5	9 or 10
Time on passage	20 mins	20 mins
Frequency/hr peak	4	2
Frequency/hr off-peak	3	1
Hours of operation*	15hr 30min	14hr 25min
Passengers/yr	1,306,900	615,200
Cars/yr	577,800	77,800
Commercial vehicles	33,700	6,000
Profit/loss	Profit est £1.5 million	Loss £2.4 million

* From first to last departures on normal weekdays

APPENDIX 2

FLEET LISTS

BANKS FAMILY SHORT SEA CROSSING VESSELS
(Excludes work boats and other small craft)

Dates: *Built* *Acquired* *Disposal*	Name(s)	Builder	L B *Metres*		Pax	Cars	Remarks

William Banks

c1940 1972 ?	*Pentalina*		23.0				Ex air-sea rescue launch. Ceased operation on the Firth in 1973.

Orkney Ferries

1989 1989 1990	*Varagen*	Cochranes Selby	55.0		150	50	Company wound up and vessel taken over by OIC. *Varagen* still operates.

Pentland Ferries

1970 1997 2010	*Pentalina B*	Ailsa Shipbuilding Troon	70.2	13.4	249	47	Formerly ex CalMac ex David MacBrayne *Iona*.
1978 2002 2009	*Claymore*	Robb Caledon Leith	70.1	15.5	250	47	Formerly ex CalMac ferry built for the Oban-Barra-South Uist service.
2008 2008	*Pentalina*	FBMA Marine Cebu, Philippines	64.0	20.0	350	78	1st vehicle carrying catamaran on Pentland Firth service.

VESSELS EMPLOYED ON THE SCRABSTER CROSSING
(Excluding short term or intermittant charters)

Dates: Name(s) Built Acquired Disposal		Builder	L B Metres	Pax	Cars	Remarks

John Stanger

| 1856 1856 1868 | *Royal Mail* | Stanger | 30.8 5.8 | | | 1st Pentland Firth steamer Stromness-Scrabster. |

George Robertson

| 1868 1868 1869 | *Pera* | Readhead Softley | 31.1 5.5 | | | Used for a brief period on the Pentland Firth. |
| 1869 1869 1892 | *Express* | Readhead Softley | 31.4 5.8 | | | |

Highland Railway Company

| 1877 1877 1882 | *John O'Groat* | Gourlay Bros. Dundee | 53.1 7.6 | | | |

North of Scotland Orkney & Shetland Steam Navigation Company

1882 1882 1890	*St Olaf*	Murdoch & Murray	39.7 6.7			
1892 1892 1951	*St Ola (I)*	Hall Russel Aberdeen	41.2 6.7			
1895 1895 1948	*St Ninian*	Ramage & Ferguson	62.5 8.8			Served on Pentland Firth in WW1 and WW2.
1877 1890 1946	*Earl of Zetland*	Fullerton Howden	37.2 6.1			Served on Pentland Firth in WW2.

Fleet Lists: Vessels Employed on the Scrabster Crossing (cont'd.)

Dates: Built Acquired Disposal	Name(s)	Builder	L B Metres		Pax	Cars	Remarks
North of Scotland Orkney & Shetland Steam Navigation Company (Cont'd.)							
1951 1951 1975	St Ola (II)	Alexander Hall & Co Aberdeen	54.3	10.1		26	Last lift on-lift off vessel on Stromness-Scrabster.
1946 1946 1975	St Clement	Hall Russel Aberdeen	57.3	9.5	12	c40	Supplemented St Ola in summer to carry cars in later years.
1974 1974 1975	St Ola (III)	Hall Russel Aberdeen	70.2	400		90	North Co taken over by P&O Ferries in 1976.
P&O Ferries							
1975 1975 1992	St Ola (III)	Hall Russel Aberdeen	70.2	400		90	
1971 1991	St Ola (IV)	Papenburg, Germany	86	500		120	
NorthLink Ferries							
1985 2002	Hebridean Isles	Cochrane Selby	85.2	15.8	507	68	On charter to NorthLink from Sep 02 till April 03 from CalMac.
2002 2002	Hamnavoe	Aker Finnyards	112	18.6	600	95	Commenced operation Stromness–Scrabster April 03.